The Despards in Ireland
1572–1838

As Recounted and Written by
Ms. Jane Despard of Cheltenham, England in 1838

Edited, Compiled and Published by
Payton Despard Fireman

The History of the Despards in Ireland, 1572–1838,
by Jane Despard of Cheltenham, England, in 1838.

Edited, compiled, and published by Payton Despard Fireman
of Morgantown, West Virginia, USA, in 2016.

Production Services:
Populore Publishing Company, Morgantown, West Virginia,
with cover design by Jenna Britton.

Front Cover: Portrait of Burton Despard, Son of Richard Despard who emigrated to America in the early 1800s. Burton was born in 1816, which dates this painting to the mid-1820s. Artist Unknown. Portrait of Laura Ellen Despard (1842–1918), a close relative of Jane Despard who bears characteristic features of the Despard family and is reputed to have resembled Jane. Artist Unknown. Both portraits owned by editor's family.

Back Cover: Portrait of Col. Edward Marcus Despard, of "Despard Plot" fame. Etched by Barlow from a sketch taken at his trial for treason. Published by Tegg & Co. 1803. See bibliography for the Wikipedia file source and link.

ISBN: 978-0-9833376-6-9

Table of Contents

Editor's Introduction

In keeping with the style of Ms. Despard's Memoranda, I would like to introduce this work in the first person. My name is Payton Despard Fireman. So far as I can tell, I am eight generations removed from Ms. Despard and those living at the time she wrote her recollections while living in Cheltenham, England, in 1838. Jane herself was born around 1790 and was thus in her late forties when she penned her memoranda.

It is clear from the very first pages that Ms. Despard is a very intelligent and well educated woman, fully steeped in the culture and mores of her time. She knows a great deal about history and is very concerned about social standing, income, "improving property", and morality. She can be very engaging and has a dry, droll wit. A self-proclaimed heretic, she does not pull her punches. Everyone gets the full magnifying glass treatment of her intellect; from "Infidel Geologists" to "cross grained" cousins as well as various idle and dissipated relatives, no one is spared except a few saintly individuals and even they get a few barbs. She also recites aphorisms, sayings and turns of speech that you just won't see anywhere else. I've never read anything like this work before.

The cast of characters is enormous. The Despard family and their kin moved in the middle/upper circles of Irish/English society and were friends with or had interactions with personages now considered historically important, including General Cornwallis, Major Andre', Lord Gage, Lord Darlington, Lord Longford, and Charles Fox's father, as well as hundreds of other personages, most with some personal detail of their life expounded.[1] There is even one instance of a woman, Kate Despard, being abducted and forced into marriage by an overzealous suitor. Also, instructive is how the extended family reacted to and survived the significant

---

1 A longer list of Lords, Ladies, Knights, Generals and other magisterial types is included after the Abstract following Jane's Memoranda.

social upheavals of the period, such as the English Civil War and various Irish Rebellions, along with their political views of these events.

Jane makes some references to her most famous relative, Edward Marcus, Despard[2], who was executed by hanging for high treason in 1803 as a result of plotting to overthrow George, III[3], but only in the context of the general family history. Sometimes Jane misses the forest for the trees.

I would characterize this narrative as a work of second tier history; it outlines the interactions and interests, not of the highest echelons, but the next rung down, below the Lords and above the stewards, shoemakers, and servants. In outlook, Jane is more noble than the nobles and something of a voyeur and aspirationalist to the highest class.

Ms. Despard's most comprehensive discussions concern her family history for the three generations preceding her own, since the birth of her Great Grandfather, William, who was born in 1680; although the memoranda recounts events in the Despard family going back to the time of the upheavals caused by the St. Bartholomew Day massacre, when one Philip de Spar of D'Esparre emigrated to the Court of Elizabeth I, and obtained an appointment to survey lands in Ireland.

In 2004 I found Ms. Despard's text in Clarksburg, West Virginia, amongst the business and personal files of my grandfather, Nathan Goff, III, who was a great nephew of the author. It consisted of 115 pages of double spaced onionskin paper that was only a carbon copy. It was just barely still legible, and my supposition is that it was typed from the original manuscript sometime between 1910 and 1930.

---

2 https://en.wikipedia.org/wiki/Edward_Despard
3 https://en.wikipedia.org/wiki/Despard_Plot

A few of the pages would scan to text but most had to be transcribed word for word.

The typed manuscript contained a great deal of archaic spelling and misspelling by Ms. Despard or the typist that in sum made the text difficult to read. In order to make this work more intelligible some of the spelling has been corrected to modern English, yet some archaic spelling has been retained to so that the text still speaks in the voice of the time Ms. Despard was writing in.[4]

The memoranda is addressed to her nephew Phillip Henry Despard [*O'Brien*][5] who is the son of Jane's brother William. It is written in the style of a letter to him and does not stay on one topic for very long. In addition, events, issues, and discussions of people's lives are revisited many pages farther along and this makes the narrative more difficult to follow. Because Ms. Despard is writing to a fellow family member she does not often use the first name of the individuals she is discussing and this adds considerable confusion. Finally, first names in the Despard family, particularly William and Philip, are reused generation after generation and this adds additional complexity.

The most confusing instance of this family trait is the fact that Jane's great grandfather, grandfather and favorite uncle were all named William Despard and they are major players in her narrative. Also, Jane's father is named Philip Despard, and the person to whom she addresses the memoranda is also named Philip Despard. In addition, in one quote Jane recites that "Three George Despards have all married three Miss Gardens [*Cardens*] in succession." Try unraveling that branch of the family!

The original onionskin text used parentheses to enclose Jane's side comments rather than commas. I can only presume that Jane

---

[4] I still retain Word documents of the un-spellchecked text segregated by the original page numbers if anyone wants to go back and look at them.
[5] It appears that Philip Henry took the matrimonial name of O'Brien when he married Ms. Francis O'Brien.

did as well, since the enclosed text is always an aside or observation.

Since Jane used parentheses so often I have used brackets [ ] to enclose the places in her text where I have inserted my conclusions about first names, place names and other relevant facts after the general term of "Uncle" or "Home Place" which Jane used as a reference. This tactic does interrupt the text to some degree but the utility seems to outweigh disturbance. In some cases Jane, realizing she must identify the person under discussion, has herself used parentheses to identify first names. Where she has done so I have not used brackets and left the text alone.

Some page numbers from the original onionskin copy remain in the published book in order to identify the places where pages or text were missing from that text. As per usual, the missing pages appear to have contained very interesting material that is now lost.[6] There are also other breaks in the text where there was nothing legible remaining on the onionskin copy; one page had a hole in the middle, which was particularly exasperating. In making what corrections I could, I had to guess at a few words based upon what I could discern from the physical copy. Parentheses identify those words. Some word sequences were entirely missing and I have used multiple periods (......) to indicate these breaks in the text.

I had hoped to edit the text by dividing it into sections that related to one set of events or a particular person so that they appeared together. This has proved to be impossible. The best approach is to retain the manuscript as she wrote it. It is a valuable and trenchant social commentary on her time and place as well as being a family history. It is written in a distinctive voice, which accurately represents the author and her world view

---

[6] Entire missing pages: 6, 28 and 36. Partial missing pages 7, 12, and 31 of the onionskin typed manuscript. It is possible that one or more of these pages may have been deliberately excluded from the typed manuscript because of the nature of the events described or the actions of her relatives.

in 18th Century England. In addition my attempts to provide topic headings based on the subject under discussion were unsuccessful because of the vast number of them and the brevity with which they are discussed. Accordingly, the text simply runs uninterrupted from beginning to end.

In some cases words, and even whole sentences, appear in the text without explanation or connection to the preceding subject matter. I can only surmise that the original penned version was missing some words or pages at the time it was typed from the original manuscript, yet the typist did not make a note of the break in the text. Sometimes the word order or choice just does not make any sense and there is nothing one can do about it but to pass on. Occasionally, Jane is internally inconsistent in her facts or simply incorrect. Sometimes her spelling is inconsistent within the document itself.

One last deficiency is that the manuscript does not conclude where it originally ended. Although Jane indicates that she is winding up her memo several pages previously, the last extant page ended with a complete sentence but the typed copy had twenty hashtags (###########) below the text signifying the end of the material transcribed.

Despite these limitations and caveats, Ms. Despard's work remains an engaging and illuminating look at her time and place.

Following Ms. Despard's memo is a short summary of the Despard family's history in America which was written by Jack Sandy Anderson, a local Harrison County, West Virginia, historian of some note and used with permission of the author.

In order to assist with identifying the individuals Ms. Despard refers to, I have compiled an Abstract of the people discussed in the text with reference to the original page numbers on the onionskin copy. In assembling this book the names and events listed in the Abstract are correct but the page numbers have lost their accuracy. Another feature of this family is that there is a fair amount of name swapping, in that some individuals take the name of the matrilineal side, when they marry. The Abstract also runs the family tree of the Despard family up to the present time, in 2016.

One feature of Jane's memo is that we learn very little about her as a person. She tells us a great deal about her family and their activities but almost nothing about herself and her journey through life.

Ms. Despard's text is not copyrighted and is in the public domain. It is published simply to make it available as a more permanent record of Ms. Despard's work. Anyone wishing to annotate, expand or otherwise make the text more useable should contact me and I will be happy to assist in that endeavor.

As found the work was titled as a Memoranda and I have maintained that designation. Also, all of the footnotes have been added by the editor.

My hope is that someone more familiar with this period of history, and Irish history in particular, will find it and annotate it or incorporate it into their work, and possibly that biographers of persons who lived in this period will find additional facts about their subject matter.

Jane Despard's Memoranda

Connected with the Despard Family from
Recollections of MISS JANE DESPARD of Cheltenham

Written in the year 1838

I am quite pleased, my dear Philip[7], to find that a history of your ancestors, though of little consequence to the world, is not by you looked upon as "an old wife's fable," but that you really wish to know what sort of persons they were and what figure they made in the comparatively small circle of public life, or the more interesting one perhaps of domestic, and I cannot avoid thinking that, leaving pedigrees out of the question, a memorial kept of the less or more particular events in every family (especially where there are children) faithfully recorded might serve for reproof, for warning, for exhortation and instruction, and for the prevention of, at least, the same errors of those gone by. The shade which affection throws over the faults of our dear departed friends, however pernicious they may have been in their results to their descendants, as well as the glorious hope of there being no more remembered against them in another life, softens the feelings in considering their defects and awakens pity or perhaps sympathetic consciousness for poor human nature in its varieties of evil, small and great, rather than peculiar condemnation of the individuals; and where a man sets about extenuating his own crimes or follies, I am apt to think it often proceeds more from the vain hope of persuading others that they are not so heinous as he knows them to be himself, or, as in the case of a failure of intellect, or the total absence of that real discernment between right and wrong, in which some writer has said "true sensibility consists", where a man goes on stumbling through life half straight, half crooked, not discerning either path sufficiently to

---

[7] Philip Henry Despard (O'Brien), her nephew and son of Jane's brother, also named Philip Despard. Philip Henry apparently took the matrimonial name of O'Brien when he married his wife Francis.

choose between, such persons are exceptions to the more conscious class mentioned above.

Our ancestor, one solitary Philip de Spar of D'Esparre fled from some of the French dominions (some say the Netherlands) and from the massacre of the French Bartholomew in the reign of Charles IX of France and his more than wicked mother, Catherine de Medici's. A French gentleman told me that he knew many of our name along the Loire and especially at Mons. A French officer told my father that Monsieur De Spar, who commanded the Swedish Protestant Brigade in Paris at the time of the French Revolution, carried the same arms as ours, and was a descendant of the Spar who was Prime Minister of Charles XII of Sweden as mentioned by Voltaire.

When your dear father [William] got the arms of the family of which I sent him a copy, painted by an officer of Engineers at Newfound, (who pronounced them very ancient) and finished them all with heraldic colours. Sir John Kinasten of Shropshire denounced them as French; and of course they were thrown away, not considering that most of the arms of England are of foreign (French or German) extraction, though many of course are now mixed with John Bull's additions, derived from his own acquisitions of wealth or honours, but the most ancient are the least mixed with such; and to go a little further back I find that the Comte D'Esparre, one of the Lords of Guienne, had his head cut off for a revolt in favour of the English in the reign of some of the Charles's of France, and as I think in our Edward the Third, in the 14th century.

You may find, in Anguetil's History of France, one of the most entertaining books I have read, as also his Memoirs of Louis XIV's Court, which is translated, and his History of the Wars of the League, which is not (so you may see that by head out off and heads left on there has been notoriety attached to them according as they wagged in wisdom or folly to the right or to the left) that the aforesaid Philip De Spar arrived, with, as it is said, his sack on his shoulder and as we may suppose some cash in his pocket, or something else which introduced him to Queen Elizabeth's notice, as well as his attachment to the reformed religion, which decidedly must have been strong when he resolved to sacrifice friends, country, the finest in Europe, and it is probable, possessions, rather than resign his faith. The Quarterly Review says "No persons have a better claim to boast of ancestry than those who are descended or those who have expatriated themselves for their preservation of their creed" and as such he commenced his career in England. Being a good mathematician he was sent by Queen Elizabeth to Ireland as a commissioner to superintend the partitioning of lands in that country, a situation in which Dr. Sir Wm Pelly, ancestor to the Marquis of Lansdown also realized a fortune one hundred years after by granting himself not a small portion of the lands in the different counties, still in possession of his prudent descendants. Perhaps Comte Philip did the same, but the Registry Office in Dublin shows more of purchase than of appropriation in his acquisitions and those of his descendants, as proved in the sales and leases in perpetuity enjoyed by the more fortunate and present proprietors.

I recollect, so long since as when I was quite a girl, hearing Mrs. Heally, of the County Kilkenny, say that my Grandfather, if he merely retained, not to say improved, the fortune he inherited from his father, must at that period have been in receipt of above £20,000 a year, but he who setteth up one and putteth down another knows what is best for us.

Whether our progenitor brought a wife with him or not, I have never heard., but it is probable he left some descendants in England as well as in Ireland, for when my father was a young man in this country, an old gentleman in London and his sister, of the name, claimed him as a relative, and sent for him to go and see them, which invitation he would neither accept himself nor allow his sister, lest the old folk, as he said, might think he wanted their money, yet he was not a fool but an accomplished well-educated gentleman of that day, popular in a high degree with all classes, and with none more than with his Eton school-fellows, especially with Lord Talbot and Lord Gage with whom he kept up correspondence and intercourse to his latest days.

At what exact period his family settled at Cranagh in the Queen's Co. I cannot say, but in 1641, the time of the extraordinary Massacre of the Protestants in Ireland, they were obliged to hide themselves for a time.[8]

[End Manuscript Page 5.]

[Manuscript missing entire page 6.][9]

[Legible fragment on page 7.][10]

…….. and there was in my childhood an old tree on the top of the hill fronting Donore, where we were repeatedly informed, perhaps (You must observe that the rhymes must be sung out with a long drawl, not expressed by the bagpipes bag.)

[End legible text on page 7.]

[Return to continuous text on bottom of Page 7.]

After this our Protestant ancestors and their Protestant neighbours lived in peace and prosperity, and I know no more of them except the many that repose in Clonenagh churchyard, near Mountrath; and if ever you passed through that filthy town on the high road to Limerick, you must also, two miles further on, have passed the pretty village of Castletown, looking down (to the right) not only on Coleraine, Shanderry, Laurelhill (the scene of your dear father's [William Despard's] childhood and of his riper affections, but now in ruins) and Alta villa, all belonging to our cousin Frank, but also on the tracks of ground once belonging to

---

[8] Jane is referring to the Portadown massacre. The Portadown massacre took place in November 1641 at what is now Portadown, County Armagh. Up to 100 mostly Protestants were killed in the River Bann by a group of O'Neill clansmen. This was the biggest individual massacre of Protestants during the Irish Rebellion of 1641. Wikipedia, accessed 6/30/2016.

[9] Which apparently discusses the civil unrest.

[10] Which consisted of a partial physical page containing a fragment of the topics discussed on the missing page 6.

our grandfathers, and still called by the poor people "The Despards' country." The village belongs to the Marquis of Lansdown who retains his acquisitions with increase.

In the year 1708 the marriage of my Great-grandfather [William Despard] took place, which I mentioned to you formerly with the eldest co-heiress of Major Green (Frances Green of Killaghy Castle) his mother was Miss Leatham of Ballyshan. (This Miss Leatham was daughter of Oliver Leatham De Mildrum. Co. Tipperary; dowager Lady Listowell and her sister Mrs. Burke were Leathams of the same family.

Major Green's father was Elias Green of Lancashire, leading persons in the country, for it was Mrs. Green who presented Sophie Hesketh at Court to the late King and Queen. Elias Green was a Cromwell's man, and died at Thomastown the seat of Lord Landaff, to whose sister or daughter he was married. The relationship was always kept up in the county, especially at the elections, when it would have been quite shocking not to support a kinsman. (Killaghy has an extensive interest in this way still.) With this marriage with Frances Green the family seem to have got up to the top of their rank in life. I am not sure that my Great-grandfather was then in Parliament, for his estate in Cork was purchased of his own (it now belongs to Lord Bantry) and his descendants say that had he lived a year longer he would have been a Judge, for he is said to have been remarkably clever, and fought hard in the House of Commons for the Hanoverian Succession in the latter years of Queen Anne; (who certainly wished to bring in her brother after she had lost her children and his attachment to the Protestant Constitution of 1688, church and state, Kings, Lords and Commons, were evinced by his will. He compiled a little work for the use of magistrates chiefly, I believe well-known in Ireland as "Robins' Contractions of the Laws" and gave it to Robins who was the Attorney or Law Agent, he was not therefore the publisher, but the writer or compiler. His descendants of Killaghy profited by it, for to the last hours of John, who died two years since, they have been considered the best

Magistrates in the County, indeed I make no doubt as to what I have heard of John's Grandfather 'that he loved a law wrangle and was generally on the right side in every case but his own."

John was the fifth generation of Killaghy Castle direct and you are the fifth generation also of Killaghy, where Grandfather was born, and of Coleraine which he built and resided at; a strange absence of all taste was displayed in so doing, as a few miles further on he had a fine place called Middlemount, with an extensive deer park, a good house and large gardens belonging to it, all walled in, and which he let afterwards to Mr. Flood on a lease for ever at six shillings an acre, since purchased and inherited by the same family. Several others got his property by the same nice disposal of his, and some by the same easy purchase, amongst others the present Frederick Trench, who still holds it. Whether Middlemount might, or might not be let to his father I cannot say, but the lease 'for ever' to Floods was his doing. Coleraine is not at all a pretty place.

In the year 1720 our Great-grandfather [William] died at Killaghy and then the tide turned which had rolled in, and rolled out in all his descendants, at first by degrees and in later years rapidly.

My Grandfather [William] was not nine years old when his father [William] died, for he had a sister or perhaps two older than himself, though only one lived to womanhood, but there are more mentioned in the will made in the year 1718, two years previous to his death. In dying he recommended his friend and one of the Guardians to his children, Councilor Hughes, for a husband to his still young wife, to which recommendation she proved very complying, but unfortunately for herself and family lost this good man within a year after their marriage.

Her son [William, Jane's Grandfather] and his property then fell into the care of an uncle [Richard of Cranagh], his father's brother, whose conduct with regard to his nephew has not come down unsullied, as I have heard of someone saying to my

12

Grandfather "Let your Uncle cheat you of £10,000" (in three days) "but let him stop there." But like many others he did not like to be advised, popularity was his object, and he had his reward; his interest carried the Queen's Co. for many years, and that of his uncle's family at Cranagh (where they continued to reside) while that of the Croasdales carried also the Co. Galway, where they both had extensive property once. The late Mr. Croasdale sold his property there in my memory, to the present Sir Thomas Burke whose family was formerly only superintendents to the great iron works on the estate of Woodfert, which I have been told is a beautiful romantic place; romance has proved to belong to the people as well as the place. When the Rynn family went there to intending to pass some time, just about the time of Mrs. Vandeleur's marriage, the whole neighborhood of the peasantry turned out with white garlands, bonfires, and every other species of rustic enjoyment to meet them, hoping as they did that their return would be permanent; their disappointment, however, was in proportion, when they found that there was a sale of the property on the tapis[11] to pay debts to the amount of £10,000. Thus has the link between the rich and the poor in that country been broken, the latter of whom are the most attached creatures in life to those they have long lived under, and from whom they have experienced care and protection; and thus are old affections torn asunder, though long remembered, and new ones not encouraged but successfully checked by deceitful, treacherous poverty.

Sir Thomas Burke, though a Papist, could not supersede the attachment to the high Protestant Croasdale, which years had produced and strengthened.

[End manuscript page 11.]

---

[11] This is not an English or Latin word so far as I can tell. It may be a misspelling from the original transcription. It may be Capias, which is a writ to take a person into custody but is not generally applied to taking property into custody.

[Legible fragment on page 12.]

Protestants amongst the peasantry. .... over from England, not only some servants, but some settlers his huntsman in particular was an Englishman, and I will here record anecdote which may now appear incredible.

[End legible fragment on page 12.]

[Return to continuous text at the bottom of page 12.]

Sometime about the middle of the last century, when my Uncle Despard was a little boy, there was a famine in Ireland (perhaps in England also) and my Grandfather through he loved his fox-hounds dearly, not choosing to waste more food on them than a reasonable share of what more properly belonged to the poor (for he was considered remarkably charitable) the aforesaid huntsman, William Baulph, used to take the hounds into the shrubbery and shaking an old willow tree there would fall the greatest quantity of locusts (when their arrival was first announced as it now in the east, by the black cloud they make in the air) which the dogs swallowed up quickly and grew fat on them. Such a circumstance is never heard of now, happily, but of the occurrence that period I have no doubt.

My Grandfather was sent to Eton at an early age, and I have heard it was a common custom for the boys to amuse themselves by running along with passing carriages into London, in which active sport he was foremost among his companions. Whether his education was finished at Eton or in the Dublin University I never heard or thought of asking, which I now regret, but I think it probably was in this country [England] as it was said his guardian Uncle was willing to keep him out of the was as long as possible. It is also said that the same good Uncle sold £10,000 worth of the Bantry estate during his minority under the pretense of paying younger children's fortunes, but it slid into his own pocket and never emerged from there again, as did also the savings of eleven years' minority.

During his absence our [Great][12] Grandmother [Ms. Frances Green of Killaghy Castle] took unto herself a third husband, a Baron Keating, (Baron I believe in …….. of the Law Courts) and having two good husbands she decided to try to one of a different description. An old-fashioned pistol remained at Killaghy in my memory, with which he used to threaten to shoot her if she did not give him, or get him money. By him she had two daughters, whom I remember seeing at Laurel Hill and at my Uncle Despard's when a child, the elder was at the time old Mrs. Nunn of Hill Castle, in the Co. Wexford; the younger (a good creature) lived and died unmarried. Old Aunt Nunn, who I have heard amused her grandnephews and nieces by wearing and sometimes shaving a long beard, had two daughters, the elder beautiful, the younger clever, (no son), in consequence of which the elder was to marry her own cousin, Mr. Nunn of St. Margaret's, in the same county or run the risk of forfeiting her father's estate to him. But old romance says she much preferred her cousin John, on the other side (a poor General) and that the love was of a very desperate kind, but in the end duty triumphed, and she became, and may be still the wife or widow of her cousin Nunn and is long since the mother of several married sons and daughters. The romance is that at the time of the Rebellion in Ireland, the General, who had never seen her after the dissolution of their love affair, being on the staff at Haverford West, received her and her children with many other fugitives from Wexford, into his house for protection, while her husband and his Yeomen cavalry played a very active part against the rebels at home. Her youngest daughter also married a cousin, a Mr. Nunn, and the general got a commission for one of their sons in the Fusiliers. I never saw any of the family since I grew up.

Whether my Great-grandmother or her husband Keating died first I cannot say, but I suppose she did, as she sold her jointure to my grandfather for £5,000, (which must have been done for fear of

---

[12] I believe Jane is referring to Ms. Walsh, her great grandmother but her text says "grandmother".

the long-barreled pistol) and died six months after, neither did I hear whether her son married previous to her death, but his sister, the only daughter of his father that lived to womanhood, having married Mr. Walsh, son of the Vicar of Blessington and Blessington Eustace in the County of Wicklow (who had come to Ireland with Archbishop Boyle as one of his chieftains very shortly after the accession of King William), her brother [William] was so often with her that he did not see her for some time, and when a reconciliation took place, the consequence was that he fell in love with the Vicar's daughter, Jane, and was hard pressed on the business by her family, or rather in the fashionable phrase of the day "manoeuvered" into it, being scarcely of age, and the lady some years older. He and his friends wished for time and a little more consideration, especially as there were counter manoeuvers practicing by Mr. Darner for his daughter with £30,000 and the young lady's full approval of Wm. Despard for a husband. She was grandmother to Lord Portarlington, and a large fortune has fallen to him within the last ten years from her family. We can only observe here in these circumstances of our ancestors how the tide of fortune began to roll out, which had before advanced, with prosperous gales, each, no doubt, disposed from Above to bring down the high looks of the proud, to which class of persons many of our family, I fear, belonged.

My grandfather [William] married Miss Walsh without a fortune and what was much worse (for that he did not want) without a marriage settlement, a thing which should never be omitted be the property small or large, and as Mrs. Walsh of Clifton told me lately, he drove off on his wedding day in a splendid carriage and four, with his bride and half a dozen grooms and attendant laqueys. (By the way I observe that his father in his will leaves his best coach and chariot and his four best carriage horses to his widow) but what was more material he entailed his estates on the twelfth son of his twelfth grandson, and added an injunction that no lease of his property should be made for more than three lives or thirty-one years, being wise enough to see the improvements that must be made by time, as those who now enjoy the bulk of it best know.

My grandmother, I have heard, what her picture hanging before me proves, was a very pretty woman, and her father, we have every reason to think, was a descendant of a very ancient popish family in the County of Kilkenny, living at a place called Howel Castle in ancient days, and now Hoel, or Hoyle, but in ruins; if so, they were at all times great adherents of the Stuarts, and sustained their forfeitures.

Under Cromwell, when chief Regicide Lieutenant commanding in Kilkenny, he carried fire and sword through every demesne belonging to the partizans of Royalty, then closely united; the family suffered more than once for the same cause at the Revolution. By the accounts I have gathered from books I am inclined to consider them as amongst the first settlers in Ireland and imported from Wales. The name Walsh or Welsh, as I have heard it called in my young days by members of the same family, has an Irish translation "Brenach" and I enquired of my old Welsh friend, Dr. Thomas, who understands his native language well, what the word meant in English, and he told me "little hill." Now the range of little hills on which the ruins of Castle Howel stands are called the Welsh hills to this day, they run along the river Barrow and into the Co. Waterford, on the borders of which river and on the edge of the two counties stand the beautiful ruins of the Abbey or Monastery of Rosbercon, erected early in the 14th century by Oliver Grace and Ursula Walsh, his wife, the parents of seventeen children, and I make no doubt that they expected to redeem the souls of their previous generation and all to come in future, by this building, although I fear the benefit does not descend on my heretic self or nephew, if indeed these good people were amongst our progenitors.

Some of the family, like many others of the same creed, retired to France, where they were ennobled, by what title I forget, but the Dowager Lady Southwell (her Lord was an Irish Papist nobleman) was Miss Walsh, daughter of the Count (somebody) and claimed connection with Henry Walsh's family; meanwhile Kilkenny and Waterford are overrun with persons of that name being hanged and transported every day. Some in England are of a better description, where are three Baronets Walsh and one in Ireland, who all, however, bear the Griffin's head for a crest, while ours carry a lion rampant with "Nole irritari leoneni" [13]for a motto. I am not quite certain of the Latin construction, but my grandmother's crest I know from seeing her arms on my Uncle Despard's plate, [William][14] which had been his father's.

The Grace family always claimed relationship with ours through the Walshes. The Colonel Walsh whose monument is one of the pillars of the Abbey Church at Bath, showed great attention to my father, as his relative, when first he entered the army, and there is a popish family in Worcestershire of the name, whose son, a young man here, some time back, we used to think like our nephew Philip to whom this is addressed.

My grandfather Walsh was born in 1655, a second son of his parents, as I believe, but whom I never could discover, for at that time there was no parish registry, and if he was of the above family, I suppose as this was the period of Cromwell's exploits in Ireland, it is possible he was carried to England by his parents; for between the years 1690 and 1692 he came to Ireland in the suite of Archbishop Boyle (appointed to Dublin) and as I imagine, one of his chieftains. In the year 1690 he baptized his first child, afterwards Mrs. Usher, in the church of Blessington, in the County of Wicklow, of which he was Rector and Vicar of Blessington Eustace. By the way he had Dean Swift for a frequent visitor, who in one of his letters to Pope says "I take the occasion of Mr. Ryves going to England etc., etc.," this was my grandfather's brother-in-law.

---

[13] I was unable to translate this phrase using online Latin to English websites.

[14] William, oldest Son Sent to School Early P.23-24. Referred to by Jane as "Uncle Despard" had a great wit. P.66 P.85

In the same church lie the remains of our ancestor of Blessington who died in 1740, aged 85 years. I sought all this information on account, as you may recollect, of the claim the Walsh family have to a fellowship at "All Souls" Oxford, but if he belonged to the Castle Howel folk he must have changed his religion and also his politics before he entered the family of the first Archbishop of Dublin, appointed by King William after the Revolution, and this is the only cause I can suggest for there being no account of who this Walsh was amongst his children farther back than his arrival in Ireland, although they claimed relationship with the Sheffield family, then Lord Mulgrave, and his descendant, the elegant Duke of Buckingham, Pope's friend and patron, and on whose son dying at 19, the last scion of the house, Pope wrote an epitaph.

My great-grandfather Walsh's wife was Miss Estwick, her father was a Doctor of Divinity of Oxford, also as I believe a connection of the Sheffield family, as I have heard from my Uncle Despard. His picture, the painting of which has been much admired and greatly abused, hangs on the wall opposite to where I write and must have been painted in the time of Charles II., for his first grandchild was baptized in Blessington in 1696, and the picture is that of a young man. It was the learned and candid "Friar Peter Walsh" as he was then called who wrote the History of the Revolution in the reign of Charles I.

Now I think I have put down all I know of a certainty about our Walsh ancestors, but what I can declare, more positively is that they were no favourites with their new allies; they were reckoned great boasters, rough in manners, with more of worldly wisdom than any other.

The descendants of the Rector of Blessington are numerous in Ireland, for he has several sons and four or five daughters.

The Ryves are all gone, they were children of the youngest daughter and were more remarkable for the elegance of their manners than the strictness of their morals.

My grandmother's eldest brother, a clergyman, was the great-grandfather of Henry Walsh, now at Clifton, who is not, as we have thought, entirely divested of some hereditary traits of character though educated from his infancy far away from them. His parents live in France and have many children besides him, his mother is English, the daughter of General Slusser, she had another son who died Solicitor General of Ireland in the prime of life; he was married to a first cousin of my grandfather Despard, a Miss Rowe, an uncommonly clever and beautiful woman, with a very handsome fortune derived from her mother, one of the co-heiresses of Killaghy Castle, and which, with much care and good management she left to her son Colonel Walsh of the 12th Dragoons, who died of a surfeit of cream and salmon; his only brother died of decline, and the fortune was transferred to their sister, Mrs. Bunbury, who married unfortunately, but her estate descended to her son, who, though bred to the church, squandered it, and has reduced a large family of sons and daughters to great distress; they are all earning their bread for themselves in this country; two of the sons have lately entered the church, one of them has married a lady of large fortune; they are both pious men and Ministers of the Gospel. The estate which was in the County Tipperary was lately sold.

Who my great-grandfather's third brother married I never heard, but the fourth married in the County Wicklow, a Miss Stewart for his first wife and a Miss Revel for his second. He had one daughter by his first wife who married a Mr. Usher, her cousin, and died without issue. By the second wife he had two sons, the eldest was in the army, and the youngest a clergyman, who always went by the name of "Bishop Blazes", why I never heard. He was a troublesome talker, and like most persons of that description, not always accurate. To draw the long bow was a besetting foible of the man, he is dead only a few years. My grandmother's mother lived at Coleraine after her father's death, to the extraordinary age of one hundred.

My grandfather [William] Despard had nine children, seven sons and two daughters, the eldest, William, was, with the second son, Philip, [Jane's Father] sent to school at the age of five and three years to the Rev. Mr. Downe's, a man of whom they always spoke with the utmost respect and affection to their latest days. My father, [Philip] for the first few years, slept with the good parson and his wife, being I suppose the youngest boy in the Seminary.

My dear Uncle [William] Despard was as a boy, as he always was as a man, remarkable for his wit, drollery, good temper and good nature; he was the pet of the school, and I remember in his advanced years whenever he was at a dinner-party he kept the table, like Yorrick, in a roar, and was the same amusing person in his own family, though he was dejected at times by the change in his fortune from his early expectations. In this respect his Uncle Walsh, the Solicitor General before mentioned, was a great loss to him, as he shortly before his death taken the arrangement of the property into his own hands, and would probably soon have discovered that my grandfather had no right to make these leases in perpetuity which he did, really appearing as if his object was to ruin his family and to enrich his tenants, and also selling as he had no right to do. My uncle was induced after this, when of age, to join his father in paying off encumbrances, and of course in confirming his father's acts thereby under the same disposing providence which had once bestowed the wealth so abused.

My uncle [William Despard] entered the Dublin University and I believe passed through it with honour, though a young man more addicted to pleasure, or rather gaiety, than the other description may include; and I have heard the General often lament his not being steady enough to pursue his studies for the Bar, as his friends and everyone else thought that with his witty talent, cleverness at repartee, his love for, as well as his knowledge of

English Literature and also his sufficiently early classical attainments, he might have made a rapid fortune, but this was not his destination. All the brothers were early good horsemen and sportsmen, and it is on record his being the first boy who ever cleared the great dyke in the College Park, Dublin, in a standing jump. He hunted in his old days, and had a beautiful little pack of hounds about the size of a lady's lap dog, the race is now extinct I believe, which I remember skipping about the breakfast parlour; that is those of the canine family that were particular pets.

He married very well, Miss Armstrong of Gillon, whose family represented the King's Co. and did so lately. They were a happy couple for his temper was sunshine and his manners and habits perfectly gentleman-like; she was, rather plain, but a good wife with a fortune of £30,000. They had seven children, a boy and a girl died in infancy; their eldest son, Peter Armstrong, was put with his brother, the late Frank, (who died nearly two years since, 1836) to school early, and when old enough was appointed Page to the Lord Lieutenant, and I recollect as a child seeing him sticking in the front of the Lord Lieutenant's carriage when he went to open Parliament in Dublin; he was a most amiable youth and generally beloved by his family as well as the poor in his father's neighborhood. He entered the 18th Dragoons, and was so far on as a lieutenant when he died of fever, greatly lamented by his brother officers, Observe the commencement of the more peculiar dispensations of Providence in the loss of this young man.

Two brothers now remained. Frank, the eldest, was pleasant and gentleman-like in company, but as an officer, a husband or domestic companion he was the perfect description of cross-grained. He was a good landlord, honourable in all things and friendly when his temper did not interfere, but I recollect him once when at home on leave of absence, getting a letter of congratulation on his promotion from some person whose office it was to inform him. His observation on reading it, or rather his execration, before a whole roomful of his relations was (as I recollect) "May the devil damn your congratulations." I repeat this to show you the man, however, he soon afterwards quitted a profession for which his rebellious spirit was unfit, and married (I cannot say how soon) a sour piece of goods like himself and a connection of his own, being niece to Lord Norbury and Mr. Toler who were nephews to his grandmother Armstrong. His wife was daughter of General Head who commanded the 13th Dragoons in the Peninsular, what one calls a real good kind of man, with nothing of the ill-natured spice of his mother's milk (who was a Toler) but who left his sour legacy chiefly to his daughter Despard, the present Dowager Shanderry. I always used to call Frank and her "Sir Andrew and Lady Acid." for they never were in harmony either with each other or with their neighbours. Poor Frank died, I am told, with a more serious way of thinking than he lived, but she was then as before quite opposed to Evangelical religion; I have not heard anything of her lately.

My uncle Despard's third son was William, he was put into the army but returned to Shanderry where he died early of an idle and dissipated life.

The eldest daughter, Eliza, a very pretty, nice girl, married at nineteen a clergyman, the youngest son of George Despard of Donore (one of the excellent of the earth), handsome and gentleman-like and beloved by everybody; he was the idol of his own immediate family and especially of the his old maid sisters as well as two married ones. But observe the second stroke of chastening mercy, he lived only four years after his marriage, leaving three little children, one just born and an inconsolable family of friends.

Eliza remained at Donore with the old father-in-law and sisters-in-law, performing all the duties to them as well as to her children in perfection as far as human fallibility allows, and one by one laid all four sister-in-laws and last of all her father-in-law, at more than ninety years of age, in the grave. The care of her son's property then fell on her, in which the poor thing was equally successful, but I think there is sometimes danger, as there is in all our best actions, of what is called prudence and propriety (for which she was famed in particular) in youth degenerating into worldly mindedness in more mature years and still mistaken for the same qualities, however, she had her reward even here, she lived to see her three ....

[End legible text on page 27.]

[Manuscript missing entire page 28.]

[Begin legible text on page 29.]

.... she no longer kept the hospitable house her husband had, or his good fortune sanctioned although the place they lived at was, and still is, beautiful and he warmly attached to it as being the residence of his forefathers for generations. Mary was capricious and non-approving. Not being entirely up to this we were on a visit there after my father's death with the General also, his last visit to Ireland. It being summer and the hay-making season we were in great admiration of the beauty of the place which won poor Pim's heart and his amazement was greatly excited at my sister and I was going away after a fortnight only of a visit. "Why not stay the Winter?" said he. He died in a few years after leaving two sons (John and Edward), the elder only 19 and the younger some years less. He did not increase his wife's fortune which surprised many as they had lived a happy couple as the world goes. Suddenly she discovered, perhaps too late, that Lacca was a paradise and nothing right elsewhere, and that her loss in a husband was more to be deplored than anyone else's. Our uncle Andrew who always lived with her after her marriage continued with her until her son John was of age. He [John Pim] married shortly after Miss Hutchinson of Mount Heaton near Roscrea, and though reckoned a stupid man, is treading in the quiet steps of his father and living among his own people.

I predict that, as there is but one child, and that a girl, the extinction of the Pim family will follow that of the Despards, except they marry her to one of the numerous cousins of Donore, especially as you have no boy old enough to anticipate a matrimonial visit for, at a future day, to his kinswoman of Lacca.

Mrs. Pim now lives in Dublin and her old uncle with her, still her sensibilities, which were not deficient in some things, are of a wayward nature as well as they might, for she was of the many Eliza lived to please although she might have claimed the precedence in this case, but the "exigante" are generally the most attended to and Eliza had obtained the habit of fashioning herself to different characters with a degree of love, prudent compliance (the result of subduing circumstances) which the sister did not meet.

I should have said that Frank, snarling, grumbling and idle, got through College with credit and when he chose to apply himself to study for the purpose of taking his degree he did it with honours and was made Moderator - a distinction shown to the best answerers. Had he gone to the Bar as proposed he would have been foremost wrangler and might have proved a useful character in that capacity as he was considered perfectly upright and just in principle and in all his transactions and very indignant at the failure of these qualities in others, therefore, instead of being a self-tormentor all his life he might have expended his acid humour better in tormenting knaves and contending for the honest with probable success and usefulness.

In his wife he showed neither taste nor judgment and Lady Trench, who is her relation, often asked what he could have chosen her for.

> "Neither bad, nor good, nor fool nor wise,
> "She did no harm nor could advise."

These were the members of my uncle Despard's family, all gone but one to where their faults are no more remembered against them.

My uncle [William Despard] himself was a religious man of his day and increased in grace by a long but not severe illness, the effect of a slight gout to which he was always subject in his latter days. He was an excellent father and improved his property by building houses although this was done to gratify his taste for building and he gave up Shanderry to Frank, reserving a very small income out of his property to himself which he need not have done had he been more selfish, until his death at which period he was in his 78th year.

[End Page 30.]

[Begin fragment of legible text on page 31.][15]

.... I could give you many instances of cousin Frank, one however, is worth noticing .... characteristic of the man. The regiment being quartered at Plymouth .... a dinner for .... one day at mess in the .... which one of the officers of his own regiment or some other had been refused a favour by his commanding officer at which Frank's indignant spirit revolted and being called upon at dinner for a toast he gave in a loud voice "The Law and the Prophets." Colonel Clay who was present desired another officer to ask Mr. Despard what he meant by the toast, upon which Frank indignantly called out "Do as you would be done by," "for that is the Law and the Prophets."

[Return to continuous text on page 31.]

Though so rebellious in his own person he was a true Royalist and would at this day be called 'ultra conservative'

The Coleraine Yeomanry were all Protestants and tenants of his father now self banished beyond the Atlantic.

He was a gentlemanlike economist and received company at his own house hospitably, and as I believe, left no debts. Once on a occasion of an expected legacy of £300 falling to him, his

---

[15] This is the page with a hole in the middle.

brother-in-law, Captain Massy advised him to put it by for an occasion that might require it, "No", he said 'it was a God-send and I'll pitch it to the Devil."

These little matters will show you what the man was who passed over his sister's son to nourish you and your brother, Packenham, in the entail of his estate in preference to him.

My dear father [Phillip] comes next as being the second son of his father and the circumstances of his youth as I have heard them from himself and others I can easily recount; but the retrospection of the misfortunes of his advanced years (in which all his children participated more or less and especially my sister, Eliza and myself) would be too painful for minute detail and are perhaps better allowed to remain in her bosom and mine, having fortunately left trifling consequences to any other. The best half of his life was happy. He was sent from Downe's school, at what age I cannot say, to a friend to fit him for the army and was always sent for every Saturday to go and pass Sunday at the house of Mr. Whyte, a tenant of his father. On one occasion the great-grandfather of your friend, Hare, then a chandler in Cork, came to the school with a stick full of candles on his back to pay him some trifle of rent (due by the same Hare to my grandfather) for his pocket money.

Whyte's daughter, afterwards Lady Longueville, was his playfellow on occasions of these Sunday visits, and the two brothers were at law after their father's death about £10,000 found under a tiled passage where he had deposited them, a common mode of preserving money in those days when specie was more in use than paper.

My father [Phillip] entered the army, I suppose, at the usual age of 16 or 17 and the steward was sent to take care of him to his quarters in England, wherever they were, a protection that a boy of 10 or 12 would spurn in modern days. His father gave 700 guineas for his Lieutenancy in the 7th Fusiliers and an old

school-fellow of my grandfather, Lord Gage, got him stationed at
Monmouth near which town he had a fine place, and which I saw
some years since in ruins. There he had the advantage of all the
best company and he was also a favourite with Lord Robert
Bertie, who commanded the regiment for I have heard the
General say he was considered the finest young man in the
Fusiliers. His conduct, I may venture to assert without partiality,
was also equally approved and as an evidence of this I shall
mention one circumstance.

He lodged in Monmouth in the house of an old merchant who
had a niece, a little girl when he was there, and on returning after
some years to the neighborhood, he went to pay a visit to his
former landlord and his wife, when the good old couple offered
him their niece and all their riches (£20,000) if he had a mind for
a wife; but he declined the proposal at which we need not be
surprised, although I believe it was a common mode of marriage
making in those days; but it spoke well for his morals and
character, and as doing so I mention it, and of which a sober
English trader of that day was a good judge and knew how to
appreciate.

I believe it was in the interval of these years that he went to
Gibraltar with his regiment, as well as with Governor General
Marcus Smith, a connection of his family and married to a sister
of Mr. Pole of Ballyfin in the Queen's Co. He purchased a
Company in the Fusiliers and must besides have had some station
in the Governor's family, as he always lived with him and had an
income of £500 a year, which could not be the product of his
commission. He was on this station seven years, when I think the
Governor died and also another very particular friend, the
Colonel of the Fusiliers, who left him in his will £700, (a
contingent amount due to him at his death) and which he never
received as Charles Fox's father was then Paymaster of the
Forces and robbed the army and nation of £300,000 in which his
legacy with many others sunk. Every matter, small or great,

seemed to predict poverty for our family, no doubt well deserved humbling of pride and prosperity.

Colonel Guyllum was succeeded by a very disagreeable man, Colonel Prescott, and my father, finding himself no longer the favourite, rashly retired from the army on half pay. He owed no man anything, but having spent his handsome income freely he had put no money by. More unadvisably perhaps, he took a little cottage near his elder brother and his father still alive, applying himself more to county amusements and society than to country business and lived a bachelor's life for five or seven years until he was 38. So scarce were larch trees in those days that he got a premium from the Dublin Society for the cultivation of some where he lived, which, like himself, have now passed away. The first that were sown in the Queen's Co. was a thimbleful of seed brought from the Alps by Lady Clanbrassil, which she presented to my grandfather and which Aunt Kitty, his second child, was made to sow along part of the stone wall which surrounded Coleraine, she was then only three or four years old. This circumstance marks the age of the trees as well as hers and I remember them, when a child, the most beautiful things hanging over the wall and nearly meeting across the road, with another row of splendid sycamores on the opposite side belonging to our residence, Larch Hill. My cousin, Frank, sold the larch with a few others more than twenty years since for £400. All the young people within reach of it [Larch Hill] congregated there, the mistress of which had been before her marriage Miss Despard of Donore and was, as uncle's wife, aunt to my mother, and grandmother to the present dwellers there. She was reckoned a good woman but extremely proud and remarkable for the well-appointed style of her house and establishment, both of which were large.

My mother [Letitia Croasdale] was daughter of the second brother of her husband, who died when she was only five and her sister three, and left them both to the care of his widow[16], only twenty-nine, the most excellent creature that could be, and to the guardianship of her elder brother, who is said to have made free with some of the timber on their property for building the present house at Rynn.

My grandfather, Crossdale, died previous to his father and prematurely, I have heard, by his leading a life common to a country gentleman of those days, more of wine that water being his beverage and which caused a great deal of uneasiness to his good wife who was a great favouite with her father and mother-in-law, with whom they both lived and remained. until the father's death. His son's name was Pilkington, after his mother's family, familiarly called Pilky, and it is recorded. that this father and son each drank a bottle of wine every day after dinner when alone, with no other conversation between them than "Pilky, your health", "Thank ye, Sir." "Sir, your health", "Thank ye, Pilky." I hope this anecdote may amuse you as it did me long before I was your age.

Our grandmother's father was an English barrister, a Mr. Trench, who married Miss O'Dowdal of Mountainstown in the County of Meath whom he married for her fortune as she possessed neither youth nor beauty and he was young and handsome if his picture does not belie him, which we had some years ago in his Judge's robes, for, having spent as much as he could of his wife's fortune he was obliged to leave Ireland and was appointed Chief Justice of the Barbadoes, where he died and where your dear father[17] saw his tombstone in going to Martinique.

So you see we are not without a drop of the real old Irish blood from the O'Dowdals, who were, notwithstanding, staunch Protestants, for it is through this connection that we possess a trunk that was once the property of the brave parson Walker, who defended the wall of Derry against the army of King James II.

[16] Jane's grandmother not apparently named in her narrative.
[17] Philip Henry to whom Jane writes the memo.

Until the price of a dog for food was eight shillings, and until relieved by King William. It contains a lease signed by his sister, Alice Walker, who might be the female ancestor of my grandmother, for Walker died a bachelor, so you see we are hereditary ultras on the Protestant cause on all sides. But observe the destination respecting property to the descendants of these persons as well as on the other side.

Had my grandmother's father outlived a rich planter's widow whom he married (older than himself), according to the law of Ireland, as survivor, he would have had a right to the sum of £30,000, but he went first and only sent to his daughter £1,500, which, with the residue of her mother's fortune, was her portion.

My grandmother was a most agreeable letter writer to her latest days in consequence of her being obliged to correspond from her earliest days with him, and I have understood he was a man not deficient of talent. His picture after my grandmother's death remained with Jane Despard, with whom she lived some years previously, but was unfortunately sold at an auction in her house, and bought by whom, no one knows. It was drawn with his wig and scarlet robes on, and I wish I had it for a relic now with one or two others.

My mother [Letitia Croasdale] met her husband [Philip Despard] in the same house that her father and mother met before, and was married in her mother's house, Great Britain Street, Dublin, where she lived from a child. She was fortunate in having a clever man, the Archdeacon of Dublin, living next door, with whom and his family her mother was very intimate; and the Archdeacon, seeing the corresponding degree of cleverness in her as a child, took pains to instruct her in some of the more solid branches of education, or rather, to create a thirst for them in herself which tended to enlarge her mind and to cultivate her understanding more than would otherwise have probably been done in those days of limitation to young ladies.

When a philosopher, like Miss Martiman or an infidel geologist, like Miss somebody else, would have the chance of being more laughed at for their pretensions than reasoned out of their opinions, when their domestic utility was much more respected than their scientific attainments, which all waste a great deal of time, striving to attain what so few arrive at in the end, the age, however, having run from one extreme to the other in her case, whether it was that my grandmother did not choose anyone to have control over them but herself I cannot say, but the daughters had no masters either for music or French, the common appendages, until my mother, who was a great idol of hers, petitioned for both and a drawing-master after she was pretty well grown up. Some flowers done by her remain with us and show what her taste, earlier cultivated, might have produced. She played a little on the guitar as did her sister. They were then considered girls of fortune. Our mother was tall and what her appearance was will be best described in the words of old Mr. Moore, grandfather of Mrs. Montgomery of Rath, that, at the age of seventeen or eighteen she was fit companion for a Prince (he was a gentleman of the old school then in Ireland, few such are seen there now.) After this she caught the small-pox, which of course altered her appearance very much. My grandmother, never having had it herself, was fearful of allowing her children to be inoculated and such was the consequence. It was a fearful business in those days, and neither my father nor his eldest brother were allowed to use meat as their general food until after they had it, and they both had it naturally very early. The General got himself inoculated after he was in the army. But a more curious custom of those days, though it was intended for cleverness, was, that on going to school, every boy's head was shaved and a wig fixed in the place, conceive children wearing wigs at three or four, a fine time for the barbers!

At twenty-four my mother refused Mr. Brabazon, a man of large fortune in the County North, preferring my father with little prospect but his half pay. His wedding dress remained in fragments in our doll's house many years after. I shall describe it for your amusement. A lavender-coloured coat embroidered round the button holes with silver thread, a buff-coloured waist-coat with large pockets embroidered in the pattern of a moss-rose and other flowers nearly as large as nature; with knee and shoe buckles of imitation diamonds, also a cocked hat; and the first Sunday they appeared in Portarlington church after they were married they were pronounced a beautiful couple and stared at as a rare show. How great was the contrast in later years; Though strongly impressed on my memory, too tenacious of such things, there is no occasion to relate, as it would be painful to bring them forward, and answer no end to do so.

Few persons are much admired for any quality, personal or mental, without a certain degree of vanity stealing in unperceived by themselves, but by many too quickly perceived mortifications no doubt intended for correction to this universal weakness of human nature so often productive of crime in its indulgence.

My father took a country house near Rynn and as the town of Mountmelliok was within a few miles and a Dragoon quarter he had military society as well as other in abundance, most of the Irish aristocracy living then at home, and, had his income not been reduced he might have continued to see company as they did. But soon after this a lease, which produced £400 a year, more of my mother's and her sister's fortunes, dropped by the death of their uncle Croasdale and. Mrs. Dunne (mother of the present General Dunne) a bigoted Papist, wisely, for her own sake, would not renew the lease to any Protestant. This was a serious reduction at a time when £400 a year would have gone farther than £800 now, and my grandfather and aunt lived with my father.

General Dunne is married to a sister of Lord Bantry and has a son, one of the most pious Gospel Ministers of the day. They live at a fine place, Brittas, not far from Rynn, but some of the brothers are still Papists and in the Austrian Service.

My father, [Philip] shortly afterwards, removed to a house in the town of Birr where there was also good society and Lord Ross' family, the Charles's and other leading persons were the first company I remember, though imperfectly, as I was only five years old, when he again moved to a cottage of my uncle Despard's building, near Laurel Hill. I never saw Birr since. Why he changed I cannot say, but I often heard my mother regret the removal from that town as she said her children would have been a proper apology for retiring from society, but having lost £500 a year by a farm he took near the town he thought he could manage his declining circumstances in the country for the business of which he was entirely unfit; and having received an easy income for so many years he was quite unacquainted with the management required for a smaller one, besides he had the troublesome failing of never being able to avoid sharing a shilling with anyone who wanted it, and considering them both, as I often do now, it is a matter of wonder to me, how two persons possessed of such excellent capabilities in every other respect, had so little wisdom as to be imposed upon too grossly by everyone with whom they had money transactions, in a manner that in retrospection appears almost incredible, had it not ruined their little property and their children's, the particulars of which it would be vain to recount. One circumstance only I will record, because I know it well, that during sixteen years of a suit in Chancery, Mr. Rochfort, a Papist attorney, appointed by the Courts to receive the rents, ran away with every shilling of the accumulation and we never heard either of him or his securities. I believe the enquiry after them would have been useless at any time. This is enough, we were completely ruined, and had not the merciful Providence who has never forsaken us, suggested to me to apply to a gentleman who has been often at our house, to memorial the Lord Lieutenant for something for my dear father, we should have been quite destitute. The Barraok Mastership of Monaghan was the result, and there he died.

But to return to Laurel Hill where the happy days of infancy were passed. His removal from that had a just cause to educate his sons and so he went to Dublin where my grandmother procured a music master for your aunt Eliza and our dear mother was our only governess.

Then your dear father [William, brother of Jane the author] entered the army and a great effort was made to make your uncle Philip an attorney, who (as I have heard) proposed, when a child, to be put as apprentice to a clergyman, and had he been made one might have been more successful in everything. My father once more returned to a house in the country from whence, it is enough to say, that, living one winter in terror, we were driven away by rebel Whitefeet or Blackfeet; lost all our plate, chiefly our mother's which had been placed in a neighboring town for safety; the house we lived in set fire to and burnt with all the furniture and my poor father received only £50 damages from the county. We were moved then to Mountmellick for protection and afterwards to Mountrath where my dear mother breathed her last after years of bad health and suffering. This is the period of our lives the particulars of which I must pass over.

My grandmother then went to live with Mrs. Jane Despard whose misfortunes would make a romance. My dear, unfortunate father went to his relations at Killaghy Castle to avoid unpleasant demands from creditors which the state of his property did not enable him to satisfy, and your aunt Eliza and I went to Dublin where our aunt Kitty [Jane's father's sister] lent us her lodgings, being herself absent. We met with the greatest kindness and friendship from everyone and were so enabled, as I said before, to procure the situation for our dear father which maintained him for the rest of his life, in which he was beloved, respected and his society courted to the day of his departure, though pressed with many difficulties, which, for the last two or three years, were overcome, but which were bitterly marked by the death of his two sons the stay and earthly support of all our sorrows, but even this has passed away, as he has himself and I trust we are pressing forward to our high calling in Christ Jesus, where "tears shall be wiped away from all eyes, and sorrow and sighing shall flee away."

The first letter your Uncle Henry [Jane's Brother] wrote after he entered the army was one of condolence on the death of his mother, as it happened as well as I can remember very shortly after he went. She had also graciously been blessed with a short visit from your father, and never shall I forget the evening of his unexpected arrival, nor could I attempt to describe the same, so fresh in my memory. With the death of our two brothers died all our earthly bliss. We began to see that all things were against us and the chastening hand of God laid not only on us but on the whole family by cutting off in succession its best scions.

I will describe your dear father's [William's] character in the few words of a soldier in the Peninsular War in Portugal, and not in his own regiment which proves their opinion to you, but which may have escaped your hearing. On seeing him pass one day "There goes." said he "the best man in the army."

[Break in Narrative]

[Orphan Sentence in original onionskin manuscript, concluding some story.]

I often reflect, I hope with advantage, on the rebellious want of resignation we evinced on the occasion of this, one of the deepest of our afflictions, if not our greatest trial. His children and widow can best add what is deficient here in further particulars.

[End orphan sentence & resume narrative.]

Your uncle Philip [Jane's brother] chose a bad profession, but with his emoluments, honestly though laboriously obtained, rose high in character in the West Indies, not only during his life but after his death when his accounts were returned to the Government perfectly clear, also to the equal satisfaction of his two securities.

With respect to his private life there it is best described in the words of a young officer of the name of Pratt to a correspondent who had been there but who never knew any of our family except himself, either at home or abroad. How the remark came round to us I cannot tell, but it is this: "It is edifying to observe the life Despard leads here." He was a man of literary tastes, excessively fond of music and all those kinds of things, reckoned very handsome; but the peculiar misfortune of his family, and the greater misfortune of being put to a profession he despised,[18] bowed down his early years and helped to ruin us all. This has also passed away into oblivion where it should be as now of no consequence. His widow has a pension.

I need not say anything of your dear father [William, Jane's brother, her nephew, Philip Henry's father] as you are well acquainted with his character and merits. He seemed born a soldier, but had it not been for the war and other circumstances he might have been a man of business as he was in a merchant's house in Dublin for a few weeks, but the poor man failed during the time, whatever it was and Providence placed him in a profession more suited to his noble mind, although it is probable he would have been an honour to the other, for there are few departments a man may show to more advantage good qualities than as a merchant or be more useful to his fellow beings. He got your Uncle Henry his first commission, the others were all purchased by himself.

You have now the leading circumstances of your own immediate part of the family, and it will be a corroboration of my opinion respecting their pecuniary destination.

When old Despard Croasdale died there were still remaining in his will two vacancies as yet riot filled which Mrs. Croasdale of Essex, one of the chief legatees, told me were intended for my sister and myself, but the old man was seized with paralysis in

---

[18] Being in Barbados, I can only surmise that this had something to do with the slave trade.

the street and barely lived to sign what he had already written. Everyone was surprised and the General [Jane's Uncle John, called General John] in particular, who said he had often heard him speak highly of us both, and had your father outlived him he would have probably been decided legatee.

The Rynn family knew no real affliction until their unexpected acquisition of wealth by him, since which they have been deeply visited, their best members taken off prematurely, and one most unfortunately.

Our relation here, Catherine Ryves, who was well acquainted with our pecuniary misfortunes, was often kind to us in sending presents of furniture and things of that kind for our little cottage, and was formerly deputed by the General to make a will in favour of my father's family. She often expressed herself as being greatly interested for us since she came to live here, as I know she had some years since before her sister's death spoken of a little legacy to Mrs. Philip in whose children she was greatly interested, having known their father.

She made a will at the suggestion of Mrs. Kirkland, in favour of Mr. Vesey (with whom she had always been in the habits of intimacy), a man of fortune near London, but no relation.

We thought there were efforts made by some of our mutual relations to keep us at a distance of late years, if so, it was no more advantage to them than to us.

Aunt Kitty was father's eldest sister. She could not be persuaded to make a will of any kind, therefore, her property, which was in land, went to my cousin Frank, and the trifle she left in money was till more trifling when divided amongst her brothers, in which the law gave Frank also a share. She had been long deaf and always stupid and we, young persons, were often imprudent in making fun of her. She showed a partiality for your Uncle Philip although she carried it no further.

Her next brother was Cartrite, who was named after Dr. Cartrite, my grandfather's tutor either at Eton or College, who had been paying him a visit previous to the birth of this boy, on which occasion he had made a will, being then an old bachelor and left his fortune of £10,000 to his future pupil; but afterwards going to Bath he met one of three old maids whom my father used to designate "Bath Hacks" who, first married him and contrived to get his money from him and then to weary him out of existence, so that all he left behind were lamentations over his own folly. His godson died very young and the next to him was Uncle Green, whom I just remember and with whom I was a favourite. He was a Captain in the Navy arid lived with my father at Laurel Hill while he was building for himself what he called "a big house" in the neighborhood, a small house still in existence and inhabited by a man of the name of Fitzgerald. He thought once I had told a lie and I lost all his former favour, but soon after he discovered that the mischief done to his little box was by a servant who thought it contained money and not me, who, however, was apt enough to be busy in that way with the boys (perhaps as ringleaders); but, sailor-like, he felt he had wronged me, and made me a present of the box to recompense me for his suspicions.

He entered the Navy as brother midshipman of Lord Longford and commenced a friendship with him which ended only with his existence, congenial souls that they were.

My uncle [Green] died of a fever shortly after he completed his wigwam [Laurel Hill] and when just on the point of marriage with a cousin of his own, Jane Despard of Donore, a long attachment and neither of them young. He left his little fortune to her, and I may add a curious circumstance of his latter days. He was going on a visit to his friend, Lord Longford, then the father of a large family, and who had promised to obtain for him a situation of some hundreds a year. He had ridden a little way on his journey when he found it likely to rain, he turned to his servant and he, too, being of the same opinion, he went back. Finding nothing to do and the day raining he sat down to make will for the want of other employment. That evening he was taken ill and died in a few days. Sometime after I was walking with my father in Dublin when a gentleman [Lord Longford] stopped to speak to him, and, on my father asking him how he did, he said, "Very ill; I shall soon be with poor Green" and so it happened. This was Lord Longford. His character and that of his family was considered excellent. My Uncle Green had a son by his housekeeper who was clerk of the parish when I was last in the Queen's Co. His father [Uncle Green] had left a sum of money to apprentice him to some trade when old enough and the poor mother behaved very well in all other respects. After his death my aunt Despard [Probably Aunt Kitty] was very good to her. I think it right, when making this little memorial of those gone by, to mention a thing of this kind, as should you hear it elsewhere, you might think I suppressed other things also.

General John was the fifth son. He left home, where he was a favourite with everyone, under the auspices of the late Marquis of Cornwallis, at 13 or 14. He, as well as the younger brothers, had been educated at the famous school of Ballitore, kept by a Quaker named Shekleton, who educated many famous men of that day, and among the rest the famous Edmund Burke, between whom and the son of Shekleton there commenced in boyhood a lasting friendship, and I have heard that his friend, Bradbourne, often appeared at the great dinners of Burke in London where he became a great man, and sometimes was accompanied by another Quaker of the name of Neal, also an old school-fellow. Lord Cornwallis became so attached to his young protégé that the world gave out he was his son, but fortunately Lord Allen being in the same quarters denied it.

The same Lord Allen being seldom on terms with his father passed many of his younger days at Coleraine. He was an exceedingly dissipated character and so was his brother, Colonel Allen, who was more particularly my father's friend as being nearer his age. I remember seeing him often in Dublin when a broken down old man. He was the collector of Armagh; his beautiful nieces were juvenile intimates, they are now dead. The men Allen kept up the character Swift so tersely bestowed on their ancestors:

"Next came Allen's Jack and Bob"
"First in every wicked job."

Lord Townsend being at Gibraltar as well as Lord Allen when my father was there made an excellent caricature of this over-grown peer peeping in at the gate of the convent. He was called in his old years "The boy of Allen." The present Lord, son to the above, is a contemptible nothing. He once on his return from the Peninsular praised your father, [Philip Henry's father William] the only good I ever heard of him.

None of the Despards of Coleraine were dissipated characters, they were, all but one, carefully educated, and, a curious custom derived from ancient days was observed there.

[There is no break in the typed text but the narrative itself contains a break here and the "curious custom" is not included in the onionskin text.]

On the young gentlemen's vacation in Winter a story teller was sent for to amuse them at night, and when he told something more extraordinary than usual and added "that's true, anyhow", the boys were more particularly convinced of the enormity of the lie. In Summer the huntsman and his assistants supplied the story teller's place, for they were all famous huntsmen and were uncommonly active to their latest days. In 1815 your uncle Henry used to look in amazement at his father [Who might be Jane's father, Philip] galloping away and rising in his saddle like a man of 30. He died in 1817.

The General [Probably General John, Jane's Uncle] passed through his military life without many circumstances worth recording to mark it, like the others. Everybody, young and old, loved and approved of him, in particular, Lord Cornwallis and his family. He was an active horseman, and when a boy or youth at home used to set off full gallop standing, not sitting on his horse, and he was always in at the finish when hunting. On one occasion, of all the brothers assembling in the mountains for a shooting party, he was the cook. He was as you know, the father of the present Colonel Hassard of the Royal Engineers, who is, as your father says, very like him. He met him in the West Indies. This was the consequence of an early unfortunate attachment in Scotland, and I once heard that after he was a married man he met the mother of his son as a governess in the family of a bishop in England. Your uncle Henry [Perhaps Henry Parnell Moore, Jane's brother] met a young officer in a regiment in India, a son of Colonel Hassard, who apparently, ignorant of the connection, praised General Despard as the best man in the world and said he was under the deepest obligations to him, rather droll in Henry's ears:

Next came, I imagine, Jane, [Jane's Aunt] who died some time about 20, the particular favourite of her father, mother, brothers, sisters, and all her more distant relatives, and, as they relate, a beauty.

Next came Andrew, [Jane's Uncle] the poor old Colonel, still alive and residing with his niece, Mrs. Pim, the only member of his eldest brother's family left in this world and the one he adopted as a child for his sole companion. His character was reckoned one of cold tranquility, gentle-manlike in all his actions. His propriety as a young officer was evinced by the approbation of the good citizens of Liverpool (where he happened to be stationed recruiting I believe during the American War) offering him a company in the newly-raised regiment. These three brothers were all in America together, the General as Adjutant-General to Lord Cornwallis. He was near being lost going out and he has given me an interesting account of his perils and escape. He was the particular friend of Major Andre, who

Washington disgraced himself by hanging. They were prisoners together for three or four years in the same town and room.

During the period of danger when the officers and the crew of the ship (which was the Adjutant-Generals and had a number of horses on board) thought every moment would be their last, the General rescues his friend Andre's writing case (which contained, as he thought, all his writings, travels on the continent, etc. and his poetry) under his arm, though not saving a shirt for himself. When at their last earthly resource a cask of Madeira, with which he plied the man to keep them working at the pumps, Admiral Cosby appeared and cheered them by saying that if they kept on until daylight he would take them all on board, which he did, and landed them all at their destination. Triumphant in the sole prize saved, the General ran to his friend, Andre, to present it (Andre had arrived in another vessel), judge of the disappointment of both when the answer was "My dear fellow, I put all my writings in the trunk down in the hold of your vessel for safety."

The General married the eldest sister of Sir Thomas Hesketh, Bart., of Rufford Hall, Lancashire, and for whom he was himself godfather; her father being an officer in the Fusiliers, and by whom he had an only daughter, Harriet, afterwards married to Captain H. F. Grenville, R.N.

My uncle, Andrew, rose to be a Major and with the same home-sick feeling returned to the Queen's Co. on half pay, at what period I do not know, but the two bachelors were living at the wigwam [Laural Hill] when we were children. He commenced the Ballyfin Cavalry, a fine corps of Protestant yeomanry now dispersed beyond the Atlantic, and was afterwards appointed an Inspecting Field Officer with the rank of Colonel, which he retained by courtesy. He has also a natural son almost an old man now, to whom it is said he is much attached. He has been his steward for many years and his life is in the lease of the farm he superintends, which probably will finally be his; it is situated at the back of Shanderry, and I am sorry to say he is as ultra a papist as his father is a Protestant. There was, I believe, another son of his sent to seek his fortune in America. I mention these persons because in your military intercourse with different parts of the world you may happen to meet the off-spring shamefully carrying a name, their claim to which must always be doubtful, and you may know who they are. Your uncle Henry enlisted one such in the Queen's Co, but when he brought him to the regiment he was strongly advised to release him, which he did, as he might have expected to be a favoured person, or else disgraced his officers. You may judge of your uncle Henry's surprise, while at New South Wales, to see at the top of the list of convicts handed to him officially "Miss Anne Despard." She was, I conjecture, a daughter of Mr. Pat Despard, a shoemaker, whose board hung out in the town of Mountrath, and who was a natural son of George Despard of Donore, an officer of Dragoons and uncle of the present William Despard of the same place.

My uncle Andrew was reckoned humane, benevolent, and an upright magistrate, as was my uncle Despard. I do not know if all the brothers were magistrates, but I think so, as well as the gentlemen of Cranagh and Donore. When we were children, six families of the same name lived within the compass of six miles.

The unfortunate Edward Marcus comes next, the youngest and most talented of the whole family. For their knowledge of the Bible and strict morals in their mature and domestic life the elder ones were indebted to a little old grandmother who lived to a great age at Coleraine, and to her private tuition they were obliged to attend during their vacations, but this unhappy man, Edward Marcus, used to detest alike his grandmother, bible and coffee, and to avoid both when he could, dreading the sound: "Master, the coffee is ready."

Edward, whom none of us ever saw, was placed at an early age in that least estimable of all noble families, Lord Hertford's, as page; he was in those days Lord Lieutenant of Ireland, and not differing much in morals from his descendants. Our uncle had a military education in the Castle of Dublin, and got rid pretty well of his grandmother and her Bible, though often at home. By the way, I should mention here, that it is said my uncle Andrew became very religious of late, which was not the case formerly, as he was thought a little skeptical.

What regiment Edward Marcus was in I cannot say, but he was a capital draughtsman, and it was by a plan of the Island of Jamaica that it was taken (on which occasion he signalized himself, and in other instances as well, as appears in the life of Lord Nelson by Southey). For this he was made Governor of Natal and Superintendent of the coast of Honduras, with large emoluments. It was there that he came into collision with Mr. Pitt. Amongst other things he exercised all the severity of the law against smugglers, which our Government would rather have winked at, as they wanted a Spanish war at the time. The people complained and the Colonel was recalled. (I do not give this for a fact). Disappointed pride burst out into opposition principles, and of course he made himself obnoxious. Whether he was guilty as was supposed, God only knows, but this is certain, that he was proud to a degree and devoid of religious principles. In other respects I have heard he was highly esteemed and liked as a gentleman and an officer. His life was published by his own secretary, Capt. Bannatyne, who concludes by saying "these are the leading features in the character of this great and good man." Someone stole this book from my father, but there is a sketch of his life by some ignorant hand that makes him to be born twenty years before his time. He was called Marcus after General Smith, my father's old friend. His fate is known to you so I need not enlarge on it. People talk of him now according to their political bias, but we may leave him to his heavenly Judge.

In his manners he was like the rest of his family, a perfect gentleman, which gave the judge an opportunity of commenting on such a man associating with persons of an inferior rank of life without some improper object. He associated, however, equally with all the enemies of Pitt's administration, with whom he was a tool, while the Government was glad to take hold of him as an example. Foremost amongst his professing friends was the now converted Sir Francis Burdett. Whether the unfortunate man was ever married to his black housekeeper or not according to his own notions I do not know, but Uncle Andrew, the only one of the brothers who kept up much intercourse with him after his change of politics, seems to think he was not. She was one of the train of black servants he brought over with him and maintained at a hotel in London, for, like his father, he thought his pocket had no bottom. Sir Francis Burdett allowed her a pension and she went to Ireland, for what, no one knows, as of course none of his relations would acknowledge her, and there she died, how soon after him I cannot say. Her son, by an ensign in the 18th regiment, and whom my uncle Andrew knew to be born before she and the Colonel ever met, was allowed to take his name, a child he never had, but this son of hers continues to use it, and there was such a person residing in the neighborhood of Cambridge within the last few years, whom I suspect was him. Many years back he ran away with a lady of fortune from a boarding-school, who certainly lived with him for some time and to whom he was supposed to be married. An officer said to our cousin Frank that a relation of his had run away with a cousin of his (Frank's) a Lieutenant Despard, upon which Frank denied even the illegitimate claim. How soon her friends took her away from him after this I cannot say, but the General, Mr. Despard and your father[19], coming out of the opera house heard a carriage called for in their name, and there appeared a flashy creole and a flashy young lady on his arm and they both stepped into it. Shortly after this he was stationed in Cork and I remember seeing a letter from a young lady there to her friend in the Queen's Co. saying she was amusing herself with a flirtation with a Mr. Despard in the 62nd regiment, in which he was then and in which he did not appear to advantage, fighting a duel with a boy of

---

[19] Her nephew, Philip Henry; his father William, Jane's brother.

sixteen, just joined, and was sent home to his friends to avoid further collision.

At the short peace of 1802 he was reduced and sent to France (I suppose about the time the wretched Colonel suffered.) and there remained, where it is said Bonaparte offered frequently to place him in a high position if he would become a supporter of him, but he, hating perhaps a king of any kind, declined all his offers and returned to England in 1814, where, in consequence of his refusal he was appointed a captain in the London Militia. Sometime before the death of the General he wrote to him as his nephew, soliciting him to get him something; his reply was the same as our cousin Frank's, that he had not even an illegitimate claim upon him. When I was in Bath. in the spring of 1814, a gentleman, who had long been a prisoner in France, told me that he knew such a person, and was induced to mention him from his great likeness to Mrs. Philip Despard.

I should not overlook in this the mention of our unfortunate uncle, he having been so doubly unfortunate as to kill a brother officer in duel, a Mr. Rochford, a member of Lord Belvidere's family, but a man of exceedingly different character, which our uncle knew and when he was spoken of as likely to get into the same regiment as he was, he gave it as his opinion that as such he must prove anything but an acquisition, which, when Rochford joined, was repeated to him by some person who loved mischief. In consequence of this there was a challenge to our uncle, which it is said he resisted as far as became consistent with the laws of honour (so called).

A trial of course followed and my uncle [Edward Marcus] was acquitted and so it appeared in the eyes of Rochford's friends, as the widow accepted a present of £100 from the man who killed her husband (a most extraordinary thing in my mind, let him have what he might), and a very strong friendship existed between a brother of Rochford's and my father, meeting with no interruption, but lasting until a short period previous to Colonel

Rochford's death, as expressed in a letter to my father when he (Col. R.) was Governor of Woolwich. I have met the daughters of the other Rochford often in company when I was a girl. The youngest was a Mrs. Magee.

I have heard anecdotes of the juvenile days of the Coleraine family from Catherine Ryves who died lately, her mother was my grandmother's sister.

Their father was an accomplished profligate who kept the pleasantest house in Windsor when (you may suppose how far back) the handsomest private party given there on the occasion of George IV. coming of age, was his house. He had two sons and two daughters, well educated and accomplished persons also, as I believe, for I saw but little of them until the old lady who died lately settled here. They lost a valuable brother, Dudley Ryves, a clergyman, some years back.

I have now, as nearly as my memory can supply me, summed up the circumstances of my grandfather's family. He did not die until after I was born, for I remember being lifted up to kiss him as he sat in a great chair. I imagine he was one of those men who never said a foolish thing and never did a wise one. He was perhaps a Whig of that day, that is a strong supporter of the Constitution in all its purity of 1688, and there were letters extant at Shanderry a few years ago from Lord Talbot, an Eton school-fellow of his, on the politics of the day, but which have disappeared before cousin Frank's organ of destructiveness which I take to have been on a very large scale.

My father [Philip] was a great favourite of his, and I think I should not omit an anecdote which displays the generous affection of his heart. At one time William Despard was not on good terms with his father, I suppose about money matters, which it would have been well that he had not submitted to arrange, as he did on this occasion. My grandfather offered to make my father his eldest son and settle his estate on him, whether he had a right to do so the law only could tell, but the offer was immediately declined with: "No, Sir, I shall never do a thing against my brothers." With four of these brothers I was well acquainted, they were remarkable at all times for their polished manners, my uncle William for his wit. They were generous, humane, hospitable and charitable, strictly attentive to the religious observance impressed on their early years as imperative, with the exception of uncle Andrew, who, when urged by the General the last time they met, on the subject of the Sacrament, said that he considered it a papist ceremony. His views are much enlightened since I am told on the nature of vital religion which he could hardly escape now in Ireland except by self exclusion. There was also a happy equanimity and constitutional cheerfulness of temper in them, which enabled them to bear the change of fortune and the consequent slights of the world without resentment, and the mortifications attending them and their descendants have not been few.

My dear father in his latter years became more irritable especially when pecuniary distresses pressed upon him with his inability to supply the wants of a rising family, but, even under temporary relief, or on the occasion of the success of any of his children, he was gay, and again the agreeable companion, always self-denying in everything and abstemious; he did not care how he lived and would have given his dinner to a hungry person rather than eat it himself. A kind word won him directly. His literary pursuits were his only pleasure in his old age; he spoke French and read and translated Latin even with some ease, the fruit of early education. His memory was surprising and showed itself in the accuracy with which he could point to and date the remarkable events in the history of the world. In those things his eldest brother and he were conspicuous, the others had more of the soldier about them. Uncle Green was passionately fond of music, and though a thorough sailor was a man of taste with all a sailors feelings. He was celebrated in a rustic song by a rural poet as:

"Despard the knave"
"That son of the wave"

The song was made on the occasion of my father and his brother having a hurling match, a rural sport that was as common in those days as cricket is now among the far superior classes of peasantry residing in Ireland. I cannot describe the game now, but it was passing a ball through a hoop; two districts were engaged from opposite sides of the country, with silk standards of different colours, attended by all the rank and beauty of the country, high and low. My father's side was defeated, which occasioned a young lady to shed tears and called forth the genius of the Queen's Co. bard. Speaking of their musical tastes reminds me of a liberty which I think no Governor of Gibraltar would venture on now. When General Smith found himself dull or his feelings out of tune he used to say to his young companion; "Phil", let us send a vessel to Naples for the Opera singers," which was no sooner said than done, and it was only lately that we broke up some manuscript written by them for my father, who was a performer himself on the piano. In dwelling, perhaps, too tediously on the circumstances of his early days, a solemn reflection naturally follows the more vivid personal recollections of his latter years. We had the consolation of seeing the last two years of his life pass in comparative ease and tranquility. His last short illness, the only one I ever knew him to have, was only disturbed by the thought of what we should do when he was gone; this I observed him whispering to himself alone, as all his efforts were made to persuade us that he might still live for our support, which however, we know he did not think at the time, and his expressions were all tenderness and gratitude.

On the 16th of next October (1838) it will be twenty years since that dear, interesting old man ceased to breathe, [Jane's father Philip] without a struggle, that is in 1817, since which, as well as before, we have seen the visible care in all our temporal pursuits, of a peculiar providence.

My mother [Letitia Croasdale] was equally generous tempered, hospitable, humane, charitable and self-denying as her husband; neither understood how to make half-a-crown out of a shilling, or how to flake a shilling bear its full price, but they left their children to Him who careth for us, who promised that He will never leave us even in this life.

My grandfather's second brother was Francis, great-grandfather to Kate of Killaghy and as I mentioned to you before the circumstances under which he became the proprietor of Killaghy Castle, I need not repeat them. He married advantageously (no less than three wives) for he was connected with the Pennyfeathers as well as the Cookes of Painstown by our ancestors with the Otways and other leading families in the Co. Tipperary, but I do not remember the names of the wives, except the last, who was a Miss Cooke, by whom he had no family, and by the second he had only one son who died in his youth of decline and by his first he had a son and a daughter. He was a money-making man, and though a barrister and thought to be the cleverest man on the Grand Jury, he was more intent on improving his landed possessions than pleading at the Bar.

He lived a hospitable life, chiefly in the old castle, as it was his son who built the present dwelling-house adjoining it. There was a small room when your aunt Eliza was there in her childhood called "Handcock's room" where a person of that name had died many years back. He was husband to an aunt of our great-grandmother, and broke his heart because his brother-in-law was so unnatural as to leave his fortune to his daughters instead of him and his son. The little room is now a landing place at the top of the stairs, but as Handcock's ghost still frequents it, or did some years back, to the terror of maids of all descriptions after a certain hour of the day according to the time of year. He has not allowed himself or his disappointment to be forgotten, and though never seen by day, continues to express his terrors on the juveniles of every generation since. He was the ancestor of the present Lord Castlemaine, whose wife was Lady Clarinda

Trench, sister to the late Lord Clancarty. A friend observed, to our great-uncle, Francis, that he would make a fortune by wives. "Oh, I don't know", was the reply, "what with bringing them in and putting them out, there is not much to be made by them." (This was fun as you may well suppose). He was greatly attached to the children of his elder brother, and it is said, would have been pleased had his son married his cousin, Jane of Coleraine, but his son [William] disobliged him most grievously by running off to Scotland while in College, at the age of 18, with a Miss Clutterbuck, who was thirty years of age at least, deformed in her person, and, except in point of birth, possessed no one requisite for the wife of a gentleman. Her husband has been described as a nice youth, of good talents, especially for the Bar, for which he was intended and in his later years particularly fitted for, and was ready to go to law for a straw, and could plead a cause better than a regular bred counsel, but, in consequence of his father withdrawing not only his maintenance but his countenance, most unwisely as unchristian like, his talents were confined to the county, where, like his father, he was reckoned the best instruct-ed magistrate there, and was applied to in all difficult cases.

He [William] was quite the gentleman in all intercourse with his neighbours and most upright as a magistrate, but, being cast off for many years by his father (I believe until he was thirty or more), he lived with his wife's family, the Clutterbucks of Bannockstown, who were hunting, drinking sportsmen and he fell into that unhappy mode of life, more from having nothing to do than from choice. He was reckoned a learned man, and loved English and Latin literature and the authors, of which he was a master. (He died with a volume of Shakespeare in his hand). He had a strong idea of the Christian religion, but his mind was, I believe, very dark on the subject; the want of a mother's early lessons were felt by him. He was harsh to his children and did not provide them with a proper education. Their mother died, fortunately in their infancy, and it was said she was prone to the convivial customs of her family, and, notwithstanding this his boyish love for her never lessened.

My father, who was a favourite with his uncle, went over to Killaghy, I believe after he had left the army and brought about a reconciliation between his cousin William and his father, soon after which the old gentleman died. The property being secured by a marriage settlement, the best part of it went to the son, but a part of it, perhaps £200 a year or more, remained in the old man's power, and this he willed to his second grandson, Thomas, whose widow now enjoys it, while the eldest grandson became entirely dependent on his father in consequence of his Scotch marriage.

I am told that William's second wife, a widow Sadleir, was an excellent woman and stepmother, for I remember the young people's lamentations for their mother when I knew them first, which was not for some years after her death. Kate's father used to cry like a child for her when he was a grown up young man. There was a law suit came along with this good woman, which, along with Mr. Despard's farming propensities and speculations, involved Killaghy in debts which are only lately paid off. But he took a third wife, still alive, (Miss Short), mother of the Rev. James Despard, who is now about thirty-four, one of the best of good clergyman, and. married to General Crawford's daughter. As I said before, Mr. Despard was a severe, as well as a negligent father. He had a tutor for his sons, and I have been told that he was anything but a proper one; they were at school, and he took their progress for granted; although so capable of discovering their deficiencies, he had experience too late when his eldest son, the late Francis, was to enter college; it was by his father's sitting with him and reading with him for some days and nights that he contrived to get him through his entrance examination under our relation, the late Archdeacon Ussher, then a Fellow and Tutor in the Dublin College. The bar was again the object, each generation seeming to think that the talents of their ancestors might be renewed in them, but, "man proposes and God disposes." Francis, like his father, was more intent on love and. matrimony than the law, and, except in making a better choice, he was inexcusable. In the first place, there was no property settled on him, secondly, he was only twenty-one, thirdly, he knew his father's objection to the young lady's brothers, who were dissolute characters, and fourthly, he knew his father to be of a violent temper and consequently rash in his decision, though never so as a public man, and, lastly, this temper had yielded so far as to make a voluntary promise, that if Francis would go to town and take his degree, he would talk to him of his marriage, which, from him, was all but absolute consent. Francis promised what at the time perhaps he intended doing and received £100 from his father for the purpose, but seeing Miss Lecky in the interim, with the concurrence of her foolish mother, who was perhaps afraid of losing him, he bought a pair of horses, wheeled the two ladies to Dublin and married the daughter, leaving his degree forever to the winds. This so irritated his father that he did not see Francis for years, nor make any provision for him, by which the latter incurred many debts, though living on the bounty of his mother-in-law who was much to blame in the transaction. The union never was a happy one. The lady, whom I saw only once, I (my dear Katie's mother) was a remarkably nice woman but not judicious as later events will prove.

My dear, kind father [Philip] exerted once more his kindly disposition, as he had done before, to reconcile the father [William Despard, Jane's Grandfather] and son, [Francis Despard, Jane's Uncle] in which he succeeded, and also in getting Killaghy settled on Francis, but there were no tender feelings, and the last step-mother did not promote cordiality, having then a son of her own to think of. The father left Killaghy and went to live in Portarlington, where he applied himself to the education of his son, James, whom he intended for the Bar; having bought experience by the want of it in the other two, and completely fitted him for college before he was seventeen, where, as I have said before, though long an invalid, he [Jane's grandfather, William Despard] died suddenly, after returning from an airing, and was found sitting upright in his chair with a volume of Shakespeare in his hand. His second son, Thomas, who was living in the same place, was in the greatest affliction for him, though they never agreed while he was alive, but James, having learned from his mother, that want of pecuniary prudence such as his father evinced, was the worst of faults, did not feel much for his loss, however, they all treasured his memory with respect, and James soon after chose his profession and became the excellent pastor he now is, although he entered college under a tutor of his father's choice, by no means spiritually minded, but a distant relation, and I believe now both mother and son are different beings. He is curate to that excellent man, the Dean of St. Patrick's (Dawson), who has a living on the borders of the Queen's Go, and gives his curates £15O a year each.

Thomas, the second son, was intended for an attorney, but his early education, or rather habits, being confined chiefly to hunting with his uncle Clutterbuck's hounds, or coursing with his father's greyhounds, and sleeping before the fire in the evenings, as I have heard his father regret, he was idle and of course, ignorant, and sat down contented with two or three hundred a year, doing nothing. He married a Miss Carey, a woman of very respectable family and lived, though useless, yet respected, being considered strict and just in all his transactions. I cannot say how many years he outlived his father, but he had no children, and after his wife's death the property goes to his brother, James, charged with a small legacy to his niece, Kate.

Francis had three sons and only one daughter that lived, poor Kate. The eldest son was a fine youth, as I have been told, until he broke his hip playing leap-frog at school, was attended by an ignorant physician, fell into a decline and died at eighteen. Mr. Roe, a Minister of his parish church attended him and brought him to a most happy condition before his death, so happy that he published a little tract for the use of William's juvenile companions on the subject.

John, who died two or three years since, very unlike his brother, except in being handsome, was the second son.

Thomas was the third son and was intended for the medical profession, and was a diligent, good boy, but he also died of an accident (which I cannot mention) at seventeen, in the same happy state of mind, under the ministry of Rev. James Shaw, who also published an account of it in his parish. At what time this last death happened I do not know, but Kate was only six years old and John fourteen or fifteen when the eldest boy, William died.

The parents, though of uncongenial temper (poor Francis it is said in particular, which was aggravated by her mother who lived with them) were agreed in a foolish idolatry of their children, increased, no doubt, by their handsomeness, and indulged in everything.

John, though by nature a gentleman in his manners, began and ended a life of dissipation joined to thoughtless extravagance in everything. He did not outlive his father much above a year. He formed an acquaintance with the 53rd regiment, then quartered in Ireland after their return from India, and especially with Lord Hill's nephews, two of the dissipated characters of the army, one of them since married to a niece of Ormsby Gore's. John ruined himself as far as he could while his father was alive (of course he and his father were always at war), and Mrs. Despard, taking John's part, lived very much with him, after her mother's death, at a little stone cottage left him by his uncle Thomas, near Killaghy not so imprudent perhaps as her husband, who was often obliged to be in Dublin on Magistrate's business and Killaghy was a marked place, and he being the terror of most of the civil classes in the country became active in bringing many murderers to justice, and in John's cottage all the idle young men of the country assembled, and amongst the rest, a cousin a Mr. Blake and a Mr. Power; the latter a man of good fortune but a libertine character. Kate at that time might have been sixteen and her parents' hopes for an establishment were very aspiring, which, if judging by the world only, might be excusable as she was greatly admired. Mrs. Despard, poor woman, professing to be very serious in religion, but common sense failed her when she kept her daughter in the house with persons whose dissolute lives were only concealed by her kindness, as also in rejecting the addresses of an English gentleman, a Major in the Army a man of fortune and character. Poor Kate did not care for any of them, but her cousin, Baker had more nerve than one. Seeing the life John was leading and perceiving that Mr. Power was a lover as well as himself and much more likely to please, he persuaded Mrs. Despard to remove from John's cottage into Clonmel, on the very proper plea (had the motive been equally correct) of removing Kate from Mr. Power's addresses. A few days after their arrival there Kate and her mother, when walking through the town, met Mr. Baker, who, taking Kate by the hand, begged of her to run with him to the Inn to see his sisters who had just arrived from the country. Kate went off, not being accustomed to restraint of any kind, an instance of which I must now recount. She had, happily for herself, a sweet temper and providentially, an excellent governess for two years, who one day gave her a box on the ear. Kate immediately set up a loud cry, knowing well the consequence. All Killaghy house was directly in motion on hearing the young lady cry, and the result was that Kate got five shillings not to tell her father that her governess slapped her, the poor thing told me this herself. But to return to my story, Kate accompanied Baker to the Inn and entered the room expecting to see female cousins instead of whom there were Baker's brother and a Mr. Sandys, a degraded clergyman. The door was locked, and Baker by threats, persuasion and terror, assisted by his vicious accomplices, hummed through the marriage ceremony, the words of which it will always be doubtful whether she repeated, as she was released from the room more dead than alive. She returned to her mother and it was not until evening that a young friend, to whom Kate communicated what had occurred, informing the unhappy mother of the circumstances. An express was sent off to Dublin for her unhappy father. Kate was willingly placed under restraint of lock and key, for she knew it was Baker's intention to take her away by force. He entered the town of Clonmel with his assistants for his diabolical purposes at the very moment when her father drove in at the other end from Dublin of which Baker had immediate knowledge, and took himself off, knowing that a day's delay would have placed him in gaol. Sandys was put up there, but Kate could not identify him (fortunately, as the act was felony). To break the marriage was the first step, which was shortly accomplished. Shaw, the Member for the University of Dublin and Sir John Meridith were the conducting lawyers. Her depositions were taken, and I think she was not called upon to appear, indeed I believe she would not have been able, as constant fainting fits were the result of every application to her to recall what passed. The marriage was of course broken, and Baker was for a long time obliged to keep out of the country.

Mrs. Despard died not long after and her father brought the dear girl to us, and on coming to be nearly of age she returned to him, whose health had suffered a severe shock by this affecting circumstance. She might have been married well while with us, that is as far as character went, but she would have had to go to India, and an overruling Providence ruled it otherwise, I hope for her eternal, as well as her temporal good. Our part would have been to tell what happened, and this would have been distressing, as we might not have gained credit for all the circumstances, as we were not on the spot. Her father, finding her health declining, and his son exceedingly wild, married, her to the first offer from a man of character, which I firmly believe Mr. William Wright to be, and though rough, I hear he is exceedingly fond of her and very good to her in every way.

I understand, that in the settlement made on her father under the auspices of mine, the property was entailed, how far I cannot tell, but it's being so has saved them a good deal of money in paying off the heavy encumbrances her grandfather had left, but she has no child, and its fate time alone can show.

I wish you would make the acquaintance of the Wrights if in their way. She has often been ill of late, and though younger than you, and Wright not much older, did anything happen, you are the oldest representative of all. (When I wrote the above lines I quite forgot that James, her uncle, would supersede her as heir).

Francis Despard [of Killaghy] had three sisters. The eldest married badly. Their father cared little for their education, and seemed to have no affection for them. I remember a governess there when I was with them very young and let them all do whatever they pleased so long as she had her bottle. The second, a very sweet girl, died of decline at nineteen. The third, a cross, little, deformed thing died unmarried, I forget when exactly.

Kate and her husband are different persons, she has had an early and severe lesson, and he has had a college education. His father is a religious, worthy man of business, a character rather rare, but much wanted in Ireland.

Once more a Mr. and Mrs. Despard are the inhabitants of Killaghy Castle; Mr. Wright, having on the accession to the property at the death of her father, changed his name to her family one.

Coleraine, Cranagh, etc. are all in the hands of farmers and strangers.

My grandfather's brother, Richard, was a clergyman and had the living of Mountrath; the parish of his family and the burial place of those that preceded him. My father used to speak in high terms of him. Although he was young when he died as a man beloved, he was remembered by many.

The living was reckoned in my young days at £300 a year, exaggeration perhaps, and of course not so much in his time. It is now possessed by Mr. Latouoh, who was presented to it by Lord Melbourne when Secretary in Ireland.

My grandfather's brother, Richard, was reckoned a good clergyman in his day, that is highly moral, charitable and humane, not given to filthy lucre, attentive to the clerical duties of that day, retired in his habits and delightful as a companion the moment he was free from pain, for he was an early martyr to gout, of which he died I believe before he was forty. I may observe here that the family in general were all temperate and deserve still the appellation of "abstemiousness", He married (I suppose early) a Miss Burton, aged seventeen, whose father was a son of the Burton Hall family, but had no money to give his daughter, who was, as the sequel will prove, pious and amiable. He settled within a mile or two of Coleraine at a place called Larch Hill, I imagine, either purchased or rented from my grandfather, which his son, the late Rev. Francis Despard., who died in the year 1819, when I was there, had brought to a high state of beauty, just previous to his death.

On the family of this our great-uncle you will observe if ever you read this manuscript, the hand of Heaven was heavy. He escaped, no doubt removed in mercy, from the evils to come. He left at his death six children, and his widow in the family way of the seventh. They were, however, provided for sufficiently to shut out anything like distress and the good little widow confined herself to the house, [Larch Hill] and to her maternal duties with my grandfather as guardian, educated her children (five sons and two daughters) to man and womanhood. Her visiting was confined almost entirely, not to the gay house of her brother-in-law, but to our sister who lived in the neighborhood.

The eldest son, William, had completed his College course and was called to be a physician or barrister; his conduct was good. He went to London, somehow in pursuit of his profession, where he caught a fever and died. This was a great calamity, but (sorry am I to write it) her eldest daughter behaved badly and married a ploughman or steward about the house. I am not an advocate for teaching young ladies house-keeping too early, though a very necessary acquisition, it brings them too much in contact with servants in families of moderate fortune, and in large establishments they are not required to do so. She was never restored to the favour of her family but lived many years as house-keeper to an old lady and died in the Queen's Co. My dear, kind father was sent for and went to visit her in her last hours.

The second son was the Rev. Francis, a very good man indeed, our first pastor, as he served the church of Annatrim near us, of which he was curate for many years, and lived at his beautiful little place near his church, like his father, in retirement, but always ready to entertain a friend with a joint of mutton and a bottle of port, the extent of clerical hospitality, and no bad specimen of a bed followed, which was generally the case, all managed, or more likely, the work of a head mistress. He married neither advantageously nor happily, a Miss Humphries, whose grandfather had been coachman at Coleraine many years, and like other dependents, made a good sum of money in that service. She enabled him to rear his son a gentleman attorney, and who, being admitted as such to the society of Captain John Despard of Cardtown, requited him by running away with his daughter and only child, and I see no blame to him for doing so seeing the young lady was willing.

Cardtown belong to my grandfather, but seeing his relation was no farmer, he made him a present of the farm which was reckoned £800 a year when I was a child. This lady, whose name was Jane, had the entire disposal of the property in her own power, which she left to her eldest son, who, with all his children, is turned vagabond through the world and portioned her other sons and daughters with £5OO each. Her character was described as being the proudest, crossest, cleanest and hardest good woman that ever lived. Her daughter, Jane, was Mrs. Parson Despard. By her the Rev. Francis Despard had five sons, at the death of the last of which she died. After the first shock was over he lived in tranquil happiness, his mother residing with him, a pattern of everything that was mild and comfortable. I much fear, however, that though an attentive pastor, as far as his clerical duties went, and beloved, as all the Protestant Ministers were in those days, especially those who lived the life he and his father did, he did not take the pains he ought with his children's education, although none of them, except the eldest, ever betrayed a dereliction of principle, but quite the reverse, but he made an idol of his eldest son, and was too much engaged in beautifying Larch Hill in those his days of repose. He was kind and gentle in his manner.

Richard, his eldest son, was put into the 23rd Dragoons by the present Lord Maryborough, the Duke of Wellington's brother, of which Colonel Pakenham was then the Major. The regiment being reduced he was placed in the 7th Dragoon Guards, during which time he attached himself to a young lady of Armagh, who, from her family connection and fortune would have been a suitable match for him. He was encouraged by her friends, and by herself, she was really attached to him, but after two years attendance Mr. Richard marched off with his troop, and left the poor girl to think of what was passed and to sigh alone. I often reproach myself that being his confidant, I did not at once tell him what I suspected, but he had no serious thoughts of marrying her. His father, had he known of it, would not have objected. The only reason there was not £5,000 for her, as well as for her sister, was that her father had no idea when he died that there was likely to be another child, but everyone knew her brothers intended settling on her a handsome portion.

After this Richard did nothing good. He was shortly drawn into (as he well deserved) forming a hasty union with a girl who had not a penny (for he never was accused in the case of Miss Olphits of money hunting), of a family and a connection of his mother's, with whom his father was not on terms, and this grieved the old man exceedingly; however, he received him and her at Larch Hill, but he shortly after disobliged his son by marrying a widow with £400 a year, a comfortable old companion to him, and some little time previously he had been presented to a living of £300 a year about eleven miles off, and he contrived, by keeping a curate, to remain at his own pretty place, to which he was too fondly, yet naturally, attached.

After this the tranquil sunshine of Larch Hill began to be hung with clouds. The new and pretty mansion was finished for strangers to inhabit, as now.

Richard was appointed paymaster of the Dublin Militia, which though shortly afterwards disbanded, was a good situation. His father was his security. His accounts were deficient, and his father paid £3000 of other debts for him, having first been seen, in his clerical hat and tall, meagre figure, to accompany him to Marshalsea Prison. After this he was under arrest for his military engagements from which he contrived to escape to America, where he may be still if he is alive. Every letter after this, to his father produced a paralytic or an apoplectic fit, and I was the first person who discovered the poor man struggling in one, and raised him up, or rather helped him to get up, while on a visit there in 1819, I think. It was heartrending to see his wasted form and broken heart sinking under the disgrace and misconduct of a too injudiciously beloved child, for whom he had carefully provided the things of this life. Never did a more charitable man exist, both as a man and a Minister of the Church.

He died that Summer while I was staying at Shanderry, and sorry am I to say that neither my cousin, Frank, nor his ill-natured wife, showed the feeling or the respect so justly due to him; indeed I remember Frank wanting me to go out to dinner with him the very day of his death, which I resisted most decidedly. His widow gave him a most expensive funeral and all ranks came in crowds to attend it to his father's grave at Mountrath; whose funeral, I have been told, was equally attended at night by torch light according to the custom of the line.

The Parson, as he was called, had had a second son, who died a Midshipman in the Royal Navy.

The third son, William, was put to some iron business in Dublin and was going on very well indeed both in character and circumstances, when he fell into decline and died.

A fourth went to America to join his uncle in business and may be alive or dead for ought I know.

And the fifth, Frank, has long held a situation in the Revenue of Ireland, but he was such a rough, untutored being I always called him the "wild man of the woods". He is married to Miss Bishop of Strangford, Co. Down, who, I am told, is very fond of him. They have no family.

All the money which "the Parson" had intended for provision for his children went to pay Richard's debts, and, after seeing him in the debtors' prison he returned to the house of the friend with whom he was staying in Dublin, and on the door being opened, he immediately fell into his arms, and was confined to his bed for six weeks. He lived, however, for three or four years after, or rather continued dying by inches, and never can be obliterated from my memory the tall melancholy spectre he appeared when he tottered into the church, where in my days of childhood, I had been accustomed to hear him regularly officiating, and where all the upper pews were filled with members of his own family, and all the lower ones with a fine race of yeomanry and their families, who have now, like himself, disappeared from the scene, and the church is in ruins. His last visit to the scene of his former duties was on the occasion of a visit from the Bishop of the Diocese, and every eye was turned on the parson's interesting and remarkable figure, as he walked slowly up the aisle. He built a glebe house on his living and had a happy set of tenantry who worked only as yearly tenants on the glebe lands, as long as they were honest and industrious, they would always be his tenants, as he told me himself that he often found them at work at dawn of the day.

Larch Hill was, I hope fortunately, left to his widow, who, I believe, still lives and has let it (else it would have been seized by Richard or his creditors), and after, to his eldest grandson on his attaining the age of twenty-five, who is call Richard, and is fully that now, and if alive, is with many other children in America with his father, where I hope he may imbibe more prudence and a better principle.

The place is I think let to a farmer and all its beauty neglected, which the poor parson had cultivated from his infancy. He was only sixty-three at his death,

His next brother was Thomas Burton Despard, who my grandfather got into the army along with some of his own younger sons. He went to the West Indies and was present at the capture of Jamaica, where his unfortunate cousin, Edward Marcus, made so conspicuous a figure. How long he lived I cannot say, but I have heard that he returned in bad health and died of liver complaint. His poor, affectionate mother, not being aware of his illness (he being in Dublin) had made a visit to her sister the day the account came of his death. As soon as she received it she fell down on her knees according to her pious custom, and before her friends raised her up, her face was turned aside by a paralytic stroke, and she soon after fell into imbecility, though far from old at the time, but, to show the force of religious habits, she had daily returns of intellect, apparently as clear as before, while at her prayers and Bible.

She rose at eight o'clock, went to her usual devotions and then took her breakfast; she was foolish then until after twelve, when again her spiritual intellect returned, and with up-lifted hands, from an immense bible, she read and prayed her accustomed time. Then, though by nature she was always a gentle, quiet creature, she was all fidget and impatience until her dinner was served, after which she went to bed, where she remained, until the next day, and then commenced the same routine. She seldom left her room. She was blessed with a most kind, affectionate daughter, who after the death of her sister-in-law, regulated and managed her brother's house with the most critical nicety. The family of Despard were always reckoned particularly clean, not always the case in Ireland. After her mother's death she married (badly) a clergyman of indifferent character, but I was glad to hear lately that he was much improved, and officiates at Sir Charles Coote's church which has an endowment of £100 a year. They have no family, not being young when they married.

The fourth brother was the unfortunate Samuel. He was put to business in the house of an Alderman Horan, a Queen's Co. man, who, from a low origin, and after being hunted out of the county by my grandfather as a mischievous youth, raised himself to wealth and city honours by honest, patient industry and willingly received one of our name into his office, where it is said, Samuel behaved so well and with such satisfaction to his friends, that the Alderman, on retiring from business, having otherwise provided for his own sons, made over the entire business to Samuel, with a patent for an indigo manufactory, with which, like his predecessors, he might have made a fortune had it been the will of Heaven, but he was the willing instrument of his own ruin. He married a Miss McMahon, a godchild and protege of my grandmother Croasdale, who came to live at our father's along with her, on the marriage of our mother. She was extremely pretty and the marriage was reckoned a good one for her as she was penniless. Previous to this her father had been killed by the falling in of a room, where, with other wine merchants, he had been assembled for a public meeting in Dublin. After her marriage she happy for a little while, but her husband soon became idle extravagant, dissipated and a drunkard. He took flour mills in the country, which, instead of attending to with his own personal exertion, he neglected, following the hounds and keeping low company. His character and circumstances fell together. She, poor woman, with a family of six or seven children, set up a school in Portarlington, from where, in consequence of snapping a pistol at him who was going to arrest him, he was obliged once to go to America, and she failed more than once, but were I to attempt entering into the minutia of her misfortunes they would be like Irish romancing, and I trust they have all passed away. She now keeps a school in Stephen's Green, Dublin, with the aid of her youngest daughter, Charlotte, a heavenly, gifted, pious creature. Your dear father [William, Jane's brother] provided for her eldest son, who was a disgrace to his kindness, and what became of him I cannot say, except that he went to Ireland a few years back and carried off his youngest brother (who had lately married imprudently, though respectably) and where they went to no one knows.

Samuel returned again to his wretched wife, became paralytic and finally died imbecile in a hospital. His eldest daughter contrived to marry a French officer, and little is known of her. His second is a most respectable governess, and his youngest, Charlotte, I mentioned before.

His second son, William, your uncle Henry got into the 17th regiment; his conduct was perfectly respectable but he was considered flighty, doing the oddest things. He made an imprudent marriage also, and died when the regiment was quartered in Edinburgh after its return from India, leaving three children, two boys and a girl, who, with the widow, live in Ireland.

Adversity seems for the present to stand still. The widow of Samuel is now nearly closing her wretched life, and has been supported by a power not known to her, and I hope is truly religious, for she has had many calls to place her whole trust and confidence in that Saviour who never willingly afflicts too deeply.

The fifth son was our great-uncle, Richard[20], after his father's death he had a situation in the National Bank, was going on very

---

[20] Richard Despard, who died in Clarsburg, WV. (1769-1853, 84 years old) He was a 2nd cousin to Jane, Son of Great Uncle Rev. Richard. Fled to America (New York) to avoid creditors of his brother Samuel's failed indigo business for whom he had stood security for in his position with National Bank.

well, and conducted himself like a gentleman, but was unfortunately induced to join his name to that of his brother Samuel in the business in Dublin, in consequence of which, when there was a failure, he became equally liable to all the debts and was obliged to abscond to America, where, by Industry and good character he again got engaged in a business, I have heard that he returned to Ireland and paid some debts, and on this occasion he married a sister of his brother Samuel's wife, who had been left £1OO by her aunt, and who accompanied him back to America, but I have heard nothing of them for years, except that your aunt, Eliza, was told, when she was last in Ireland, that Samuel Despard sold silk In New York.

I should mention that he had a fourth son, the Rev. Samuel Despard, who was a credit and a consolation to his mother and family. For many years he has been, and still is, curate to Mr. Vignolles and tutor to his son.

This is as far as my father's memory and my own can supply the chief circumstances attending the descendants of the three sons of our great-grandfather, who was a good, and, as I have been told, a wise man, and whom it pleased God to take away, humanly speaking, so early.

His father and younger brother remained at Cranagh, about two miles from Coleraine when we lived at Killaghy, he had sisters, how many I cannot say, but one is married to Mr. Philips of the Queen's Co. and is the female ancestor of that family there, and of Mrs. Mitford, whose son you saw at Clifton. Mrs. Philips died at Larch Hill, at her nephew's, the clergyman, and by that was then, I suppose a widow. I think there was another, a Mrs. Palmer.

There are varieties of tombstones in the churchyard at Cranagh, near Mountrath, over some of which, especially those of our grandfather and grandmother, the walls of the old church have fallen, which tell of generations of Cranagh far beyond what I have gathered.

The old walls of the house, which I remember, have disappeared and a farm is in its place. Notwithstanding, the ghosts of our ancestors still hold the tenure and were so little ecclesiastical as to torment a clergyman's widow and daughter who inhabited the modern edifice, when I was last at Larch Hill, and which I heard a young lady declare most injudiciously in the presence of Richard Despard's two little boys, to be the case; but I suspected they were spirits of more material substance, and I think I may record an anecdote of one of our ancestors there. He was a magistrate and, as such, took information against a Mr. Lambert (an "ought to be" gentleman, and an ancestor of the present Lord Cavan, who still holds an estate adjoining) for receiving stolen cattle at his house, and which was proved against him, although as it appears, with no disgrace to his descendants, whose morals, I fear, have not raised with their rank.

It would be difficult to find in the rubbish in Clonenagh churchyard what year our great-grandfather died, but his second son, Richard, settled, or rather remained, at Cranagh, which had a good property annexed, and especially one of £8OO a year, which his family lost in a lawsuit with the Duke of Chandos, who gained this along with a good deal more belonging to other persons in the county. This Richard was my grandfather's guardian, as mentioned before (not very honourable). He married a Miss Kent of the County Tipperary, with a good fortune, which was still in the family a few years back, and I believe it is still. He was no spendthrift, as it appears, being rather willing to take more than his own, and left his eldest eon a very good fortune. He had three sons and two daughters, the eldest of whom married Miss Weldon of Kilmarony near Athy (her nieces are now Lady Erne and Mrs. Dean Trench). They had no children, so he set about to spend gaily like his cousin of Coleraine, but less usefully, as electioneering for the Parnell's civilizing and improving his country were the extensive objects of the squanderers there, whilst company and conviviality (ill named) was the order at Cranagh. Both kept a train of servants and carriages, and both always drove four horses, the habits of one displayed an English education, those of the other that of his own country.

Many years ago Mrs. Taylor, sister of the present Lord Clancarty, told me that the dearest friend she had was Mrs. Despard of Cranagh and her husband [Richard] was the pleasantest man in the world, but added an expression in a whisper which astonished me "But he was a drunken devil."

Cranagh being divided from the high road by a large lawn he provided himself with a large trumpet, which he sounded to announce dinner to every person going by, as well as to his guests. Indeed I believe in those days travelers were privileged to turn in and dine. He was fond of my father [Philip] when a little boy, and to keep the balance even, whenever my elder uncle got a new pony, a new whip or a new pair of boots, Phil was sure to have a present of some kind from his relation at Cranagh; he was a bad child's guide, however. He was killed by a fall from a horse, his bead coming in contact with the only stone on the road and his brains were scattered on it.

His brother, George, succeeded to his debts rather than to his property. I think Donore (which George's grandson now inhabits) was built ....

He [George] married Miss Carden, the ancestress of the Donore branch of the family. Sir John Carden, her grandfather, had originally been a butcher in the town of Roscrea, a circumstance perpetuated by the following anecdote. He grew so rich that he was said to have found money and he reared a son a gentleman, whom he then proposed in marriage to Miss Warburton of Garryhinch, one of the thick-blooded antiquities, but not so prosperous. When her father observed; "Sir, you have not blood," "No, Sir' said Mr. Garden, "but I have fat." So the mixture being agreed upon, the daughter of that marriage was Mrs. George Despard of Donore.

I daresay George's alliance was a happy one, but not a healthy one, for out of sixteen children or more, only eight survived to mature or elderly years rather than to advanced old age, and every one of them preceded their father to the grave, except one, he belonging to the temperate class, living to ninety, the remainder all dying of gout or liver complaint common to the Cardens, and increased by the eldest son marrying his own cousin-german, afterwards the mother of a numerous family. She died when her eldest child, Gertrude, was not sixteen, on whom the whole duties of her father's house and young family fell, duties which she fulfilled in the most exemplary manner, never marrying, but looked up to by all persons as a pattern. Partiality will not be suspected, as I cannot vouch for this myself, though I remember her well, as she lived to sixty years of age, but the last time I saw Miss Ponsonby (one of the old curiosities of Llangollen) she mentioned her in far higher terms than I do, and also her next sister, Elizabeth.

There were six daughters in the family and two sons. Two of the former were married, Mrs. Favien and Mrs. Twigg. One of the others was to have been married to her cousin, our sailor uncle, Green, who died. Judith, another daughter was thought to be a little flighty, and Elizabeth always lived with her uncle Pigott, father of the present Sir George Pigott who married our cousin, Mary Croasdale. The eldest son, George, was an officer of Dragoons, and married his own cousin german, Miss Carden of Lismore in the Queen's Co. He left the army and settled in the village of Castletown, about two miles from his father's, after a few years. Being of a gouty and bilious constitution, and the father of four infants, he caught the whooping cough from them and, after a long illness, died. Not being at the time on kind terms with his father or excellent brother, he did an act which he thought would show his feelings without ever being brought into practical effect; he left his fortune to his brother-in-law,

Lieutenant-Col. Garden of the 17th Dragoons, in case of the (apparently improbable) decease of his four children, which took place in the course of four years, the eldest being the last to go off with water on the brain. The widow survived him some years.

George was, of course, a magistrate of the county, and I shall here recount a circumstance, in which he was concerned, that displays the spirit of popery with all its effects on the attached peasantry. A Protestant of the name of Thompson kept a respectable shop in the village of Castletown, in which his sister was his partner. Thompson came home one day from the fair of Mountrath with eight guineas in his pocket, and meeting the priest, Father Kearns, on the road, brought him in to dine with him in his little back parlour behind the shop. Thompson being fatigued, fell asleep, when the priest slyly putting his hand in the man's pocket, stole his eight guineas. His sister, who was attending the shop, saw the transaction through a little window in the door of the room, and went to George Despard to lodge information, who immediately issued a warrant to apprehend the priest, and the constables were leading him off next day to the gaol of Maryborough, when a mob arose which shortly covered the road, and as they had to pass George Despard's house going out of the village, he came out and swore he would shoot the first man who attempted to rescue the priest. "Shoot him, kill him," shouted a hundred voices, "Our priest shall not go to gaol."

The finale was, from having no military, he was obliged to run for his life and Father Kearns was rescued. This was previous to the illness which sent him to his grave but years after I have heard it asserted by servants and persons of that description that his severe illness and death were the consequence of his arresting a priest. That this was the belief of the people is shown by the following anecdote. A man begged to see him one day, and he was ushered into his sick chamber, where he lamented over him with tears as well as with many affectionate expressions to him and his family, and having overcome his fears of offending, he ventured to prescribe a cure for all his ailments. "What is that, my good fellow?" said George. The poor clown, falling down on his knees with his hands clasped, begged him to send for the priest and say one word to him (that meant to apologize) and you will get well directly. The prescription, as you may well believe was neglected, however, the tide of opinion running against the priest, who everybody knew had robbed the man, he was obliged to leave that county, and was soon after taken by the late Francis Despard, then a youth, in the act of leading on and exciting the people to rebellion. He was committed to the gaol of Clonmel by Frank Despard, and shortly afterwards hanged. The woman, Thompson, dying suddenly, was universally supposed to have been poisoned.

On the death of the children Colonel Garden [possibly Carden] compromised the property with Richard Despard, brother of George, but, having made no will, nor married, at his death the property thus obtained in exchange, together with whatever landed property he had, went to a distant relation, whom he did not know and cared for less; conscience ought to have induced him to return to the family what he knew came to him on a bad, foundation. He was reckoned a man of high character and honest, but there are slippery principles on a sandy soil.

By the unexpected decision of the lawsuit mentioned before and by which the Duke of Buckingham derives £20,000 a year from the Queens Co., Colonel Garden lost £100 a year; the suit is said to have lasted for forty years.

The second son of George Despard was the Rev. Richard Despard. He married our cousin Eliza, whom I mentioned before and was father to the present William Despard of Donore, (an ultra-conservative and an active magistrate) to George and to Gertrude, the latter born at her father's death, and now married to her first cousin, James Twigg. They have a daughter deaf and dumb, the frequent consequence of so close a relationship.

William of Donore married Letitia Sandea, a niece of the late Mr. Croasdale of Rynn and has six sons and four daughters. He was born in 1798. His father was the idol of his family and friends, possessing all the endearing qualities of domestic and social life. His grandfather Garden left him and one sister £1,500, and £100O to the other sisters. He (the Rev. Richard Despard) had the whitest teeth and blackest eyes (a beautiful contrast) that family was remarkable for both.

His son, George, lost the sight of one eye when an infant. He was put into the 53rd regiment by his guardian, the present Lord Maryborough, and leaving it on account of his health, was placed in the constabulary in Ireland as a stipendiary Magistrate, where he makes a very good figure, according to the public papers, and is a determined conservative in Lord Normanby. He is married to Gertrude Garden, also a distant cousin, and sister to the Carden who succeeded to Colonel Garden's property. Another sister, Maria, is married to Henry Sandea, brother of Mrs. William of Donore. William's grandfather had another brother, Lambert, who, I have heard, was considered flighty and died unmarried. I suppose he was named after his father's neighbour, Lord Cavan, the "cow stealer."

Three George Despards have all married three Miss Gardens [Cardens] in succession. The latter was all for love I understand and was a very happy one, as were the others also except for bringing disease into an uncommonly healthy family.

Two daughters spring from Cranagh. The first was married to my mother's eldest uncle of Rynn, which marriage was productive of a strong likeness between that family and the Donore.

The second daughter was married to Dr. Carr, the Chaplain of the House of Commons in Ireland and Rector of Aghadoe near Cranagh. Their only daughter was Mrs. Twigg, late of Merrion Square, Dublin, who lived and died a card-playing votary of the world. Of her two brothers, the Mr. Carrs, I know but little,

74

except that the son of the eldest brother married a niece of Warburton, Bishop of Limerick. He was himself a clergyman with a good living annexed to a nice property. She turned out a most infamous creature, and ruined him, for I remember hearing when I was leaving Ireland that he was ruined. She had a settlement of £4OQ a year, but I never heard that the property was settled on her children. Carr was reckoned a weak man and his appearance did not belie the imputation. Thus you see that the descendants of the Despards are equally doomed, male and female, to look downwards, some way or other.

Old Dr. Carr lost his first wife (Miss Despard) early, and you may judge what sort of a man he was, when he is said to have carried his dead infant in a portmanteau behind his servant from Dublin to Aghadoe in order to save the expense of burying it anywhere but in his own vault. Many other anecdotes I have heard of the man quite as disgraceful, by which we need not be surprised that the place of his descendants is no more to be found. Ahgadoe and the living were still belonging to the grandson, though he was in gaol in the year 1819.

The present Croasdales of Rynn are the descendants of the other daughter. They were all good and highly respectable, and happy though under a pecuniary cloud. Since their great acquisition of wealth by the death of Despard Croasdale, which happened when you were a little boy, they have been visited with many trials. Four of the present generation have died, and a fifth, Thomas Croasdaile, is now in London and is not expected to live. A distant relation, Despard Croasdaile, by the extravagance of his father and mother, was left an orphan with one or two mere boys unprovided for. He, being very young, was taken under the care of an old woman, a Mrs. Honor, a relation. Her geographical knowledge was not extensive as I have heard she enquired of her young protege "Dear Honey, Despard, will you go all the way to Minorca in a post-chaise?"

My grandfather, [William] Despard, got him [Despard Croasdaile] his commission, and he possessed a small property at the back of Rynn under £1OO a year, which he left to the family there. It is said that he early showed himself ungrateful by going against my grandfather [William] at an election, so far as giving his vote to the opposite party to that which my grandfather expected. Let that be as it may, my grandfather, Croasdaile was kind and hospitable to him when he and his cousin at Rynn were at variance and did not speak, and there is no appearance of any open reconciliation having taken place between them, although he left him and his children such wealth, and passed over the family of him who first set him out in the world. However, his character for upright, straightforward honour and honesty was unblemished, and must have been so early in life. Croasdaile left his wife besides a jointure of £2,000 a year, £12,000 in her own power, it was said to enable her to provide for the reduced children of her brother, Colonel Fitter. It is also said that he did not know the full extent of his wealth when he died. Some of the Cranagh family stood sponsor for him, by which he obtained the baptismal name.

There are many generations and individuals of our family beyond what I have heard or enquired about, with the exception of my once having run through the old churchyard at Clonenagh and seen numerous tombstones with the name on them, but I was too young to mind any of them much, except a John Despard, aged thirty years and his wife, Mary, aged twenty-two and both I think died in the same year. This circumstance alone attracted my attention and fixed it on my memory, the date was 16--, further I cannot say, but I know by their marriage the family had numerous connections in the adjoining counties, and there is an Edward Despard mentioned in my great-father's marriage settlement who was not so near a relation as an uncle. Who he was I cannot say, as I have said before William Wellesley Despard is the only one left in the Queen's Co., and my dear Kate of Killaghy in the County Tipperary, how long they may stand Heaven only knows; the latter had no child, William has six sons and four daughters. His mother educated him to the best of her judgment, and would have had him follow the steps of his father by taking orders. She had a private tutor for him as he was idle and loved horses better than books, therefore he did not take his degree not finish his studies, as he told his guardian, Lord Maryborough, when speaking to him on the subject, who asked whether he thought his life was an idle one, adding that no one worked harder than he did (for he was then in the Ministry), that he would not leave old Donore for £5,000 a year; he laid aside his foolishness, however, and married, since which he has led a quiet life at old Donore. He has ten children at thirty-eight; old Councilor Sandes, his wife's uncle living with him, and being an acquisition to him in every way, and he, as well as his brother, George, being ultra conservatives, are steering themselves cleverly as magistrates in their difficult duty in Ireland. It is said that men have more than once stopped at the gate of Donore to consult whether they should go up and despatch him, or frighten him out of the country, but, as they say in Ireland, their hearts failed them, in either sending him out of the world or banishing from the place the family who had stood by them so long. He has had many whispers from those most concerned to restrain the ebullition of hid Protestantism, and his steward was served with a notice some years hack for both him and his master to quit or take the consequence, yet they have stood their ground fearlessly. One season, however, his men refused to work for him, and this was as it were to stop the supplies, and he was then near being in a bad way, until one of the men who was longing to break his vow, yet to satisfy his conscience, went privately to Mr. Hawksworth and told him that if any man came forward and broke the ground, the labourers would all follow, upon this Hawksworth went himself, took the plough, and was immediately followed by all the men. If there were not such loop-holes for these poor, deluded creatures to escape through, the country might, if possible, be worse than it is, and none but radical magistrates allowed to act; a perfectly new race, although the man who does strict justice is always most liked. George lives in Co. Meath.

In summing up the memoranda, as I may call them, of what I have known of some of our family, and have heard of others, I think I may say that, although I have recorded irregularities, to call them no worse, I cannot set down any of them as bad men, with the exception of the unfortunate Edward Marcus, and Samuel Despard, the merchant and his eldest son, Richard, whom your father [William, Jane's brother] got into the army; I hope God may have touched his heart, if he is still alive. He [Richard] took his younger brother, Philip, who married imprudently, but respectably, a Miss Roe of Tipperary, to America, (I believe Kentucky) some years back. He was well-conducted, but had no energy in his character, however, a new position calls forth unexpected efforts, but we have heard nothing of them since they went. His cousin, Richard, the unfortunate son of the clergyman, was in New York some years back with a numerous family. His uncle, Richard, an honourable, upright man, was also in New York some years ago, driven there by the misconduct of his brother Samuel, but is probably dead,[21] as that family is not long lived, indeed they may all be so for ought I know, but some accident may bring you in contact with the descendants they have left, and. this paper will tell you who they are, Those in America are all from Larch Hill -that sweet, pretty place, bereft of those with whom a few years ago it was an idol, and with only a nominal owner. The affectionate resemblance which so many of the peasantry still retain in that part of the Queen's Co. still called the "Despard's country", proved that no acts of pression strain their memory, or left their memory behind them.

Whether William and his numerous family are to be the seed of revived generations time only will show. I am told they are a fine family, but the chastening hand of heaven has been laid upon all of late years and none have escaped as appears by this little

---

[21] This Richard is I believe the editor's ancestor who lived to be 84 and died in Clarksburg, WV, in 1863.

manuscript. Your dear father, [Philip] the last time he was in Ireland, about a year before he fell, went to Shanderry to pay his cousin Frank a visit, and passing the gate of Larch Hill, the scone of his infancy, stopped to contemplate it, and shed tears on thinking it could never be his, for he loved the place dearly. He also dined with the happy pastor, also a Francis Despard.

Should I call to mind anything more of the immediate family before I send this, which might please or amuse you, I will add them, and I will put a few anecdotes which may be characteristic of persons in days gone by. I have annexed a list of extensive property in land which your ancestors possessed which now give the appelation of men of fortune to their separate owners.[22] I never heard what the politics of the family were at the time of Cromwell, I believe they were monarchical, although their just dislike and personal dread of popery from ancient experience might almost excuse their upholding anything that was Protestant, but there was no forfeiture of any kind that I have heard of, and the proscription during the short visit of James II, to Ireland did not produce anything but a temporary flight, soon relieved by William of glorious memory. On the other hand, the Walshes were entirely ruined, first by Cromwell, then by the Act of Indemnity of their friend Charles II., and finally, by their adherence to the Stuarts, and, as I think, to popery in the reign of King William, at which period our great-grandfather, Walshe, came over as chaplain to the first Archbishop Boyle, appointed to Dublin after the Revolution of 1688. The good man's bones rest in the churchyard of Blessington, Co. Wicklow, the living into which he was inducted shortly after his arrival. He had Dean Swift for his friend and neighbour, and I am rather inclined to think he belonged to the family of Hewell Castle, but had abjured their politics and their religion together, which I almost imagine was the reason that his birthplace was unknown to his children, and the parish he was born in is impossible to trace. All, the latter, however, claim the Sheffield connection, which belonged

---

[22] This document did not accompany the onionskin manuscript found by the editor.

alone to the Hewell Castle Walshes, and the late Mr. Sheffield Grace claimed the Despards through the same connection (the Walshes). Queen Anne, who certainly liked her father's adherents had a Walsh for her Master of the Horse -Pope's earliest friend and critic, and it is possible, a concealed papist. The Greens of Killaghy Castle, were, on the other hand, firm, determined Cromwellians, and. even when I was a girl I remember the Aliens disputing about the beheading of King Charles. The late Lord Allen and his wife had a pension between them of £15000 a year,

My great-grandmother [Ms. Frances Green of Killaghy Castle] I heard was a beauty, and liked matrimony, it seems, as she had three husbands. The second sister, Lady Levinge, was firm in every way. She had a bad husband, but was able to take her own part, and being badly used who went to Dublin and consulted her lawyer, who told her she might get possession of her own fortune from him, and was advised if she could provoke her husband to strike her before witnesses, she would succeed in that wish. Quite equal to the encounter she posted back to the country, and soon obtained as legal a drubbing as her bones could bear, and of course was put in possession of her property. Her son, the late Sir Richard Levinge, a good man I believe, died suddenly in the town of Chester. He left several children, the eldest, Sir Richard, lives on his property in Westmeath, and is married to Miss Parkins, sister to Lord Rancliffe and the Princess Polignac. The descendants of a great-aunt, (Lady Levinge) by her second son, Richard, possessed the property in county Tipperary. Her husband, after her death, married his cook, and I have heard my father say that he had two sons and two daughters by her, patterns of beauty like their mother. I have also heard that the old Lady Levinge was so fat that she once stuck in a sedan chair at her sister, Lady Allen's door, and could not get out, her rage at being so enthralled being much increased by seeing her two nephews, my father [Philip] and his cousin Allen, peeping at her from the corner of the street and not attempting her relief, although her shut fists were upraised threatening the boys with all her might; perhaps the squeezing may have hurried, her out of the world. One of her daughters did not behave well, somehow or other not very surprising with such parents.

Lady Allen was a gentle creature and left two sons, two daughters and two beautiful grand-daughters, whom I mentioned before. Of another sister I never heard anything but that her immediate descendants, the Moore's, live in the County of Cork and Tipperary. Mrs. Rowe, the youngest of the five, left two daughters, one of whom was killed by jumping out of a carriage while the horses were running away. The other married my grandmother Despard's brother, who was Solicitor General of Dublin when he died and his property descended to her grandson, Bunhury, who has squandered away every shilling of it as I mentioned before. These are five co-heiresses of Killaghy Castle, a memento of whom, an immense oak tree with five great arms - was felled to the ground with peculiar bad taste by the late Mr. Despard. The axe had not been idle among their descendants.

The life of a military man in days gone by seems to have been one of fun and frolic, and I recollect many curious anecdotes of such from my father and uncle Capt. Shears, father to the unfortunate man who married Mrs. General Despard's sister and who shot himself in a hotel Cheltenham many years back, was in the Fusiliers with my father. The Coleraine men were all peaceable, but Captain Shears, going into a hotel in England one day, accompanied fortunately by my father,[Philip] and not seeing anyone, roared out .... Upon which the waiter informed him that none but an ignorant Irishman could suppose the word ....could answer him. Capt. Shears flew at him, and, but for his companions, would have made him feel the full weight of an Irishman's arm. At another time Capt. Shears, wanting money from his elder brother who was a man of fortune in Co. Cork, and being refused, he advertised the family bank to be sold, which, by some accident, happened to be his property............ this had the desired effect. The two sons of this elder brother were hanged at the rebellion in

Ireland and the only child of one of them, Miss Shears, is married to a distant relation of ours, a Mr. Butler of Edmondbury in the county Kilkenny.

To torment the Jews at Gibraltar was a daily frolic, and I have heard it cost another officer of the 7th Fusiliers six shillings a week for rotten eggs to pelt the Jews. Dare any officer so amuse himself now-a-days?

My father [Philip] used in summer frequently to accompany General Smith into Spain, where they not infrequently took up their residence in a convent, sometimes for months at a time and often in his old age did he talk of the tranquil, simple life of the monks as enviable, had not the cowl covered the wily Jesuit. There was also a famous Donna at that time, a woman of rank and a belle of beauty, who used to receive the visits of all the British officers on condition of their bowing to the Mana del' Cavina which hung over the couch on which she reclined, on their first entrance to her levee.

My uncle Despard had his campaigning at home with equal ease and higher promotion, for, in writing to his brother he told him of the Volunteer Corps then raising in Ireland, adding: "I am Colonel, for who would be less when he promotes himself?"

##[23]

[End Manuscript]

---

[23] These hashtags were typed at the end of the original onionskin text. Some pages of the original must have been lost prior to transcription or not included in the typed copy.

"The Despards," by Jack Sandy Anderson

Many people looked upon Western Virginia as a land of opportunity in the earlier years of the nineteenth century and settled in one of its counties. Among them was Richard Despard, who established his home in Clarksburg where he became a well-known and influential citizen.

Born and reared in Ireland, he emigrated to New York in 1803. A year later he went to Ireland to marry Diana McMahon, and soon thereafter returned to New York with her. In 1813, sight unseen, he purchased 1000 acres of land lying along Elk Creek; and in the 1820's he and his wife and children left New York and settled in Clarksburg.

Soon after their arrival, Mrs. Despard opened a seminary for young ladies. Subjects taught included orthography (spelling), grammar, reading, writing, arithmetic, history, astronomy, botany, French, Italian, and music. For the artistic, there were classes in oil painting, velvet painting, and painting with water colors. And there were classes in sewing that featured not only plain sewing but also embroidery, tambour, and other ornamental needlework. The enrollment was limited to twenty students. It is not known just when the seminary opened, but it was in existence in 1824.

The Despards liked their home in Western Virginia. in ways they were reminded of faraway Ireland, especially when the hills and valleys were covered in green. They liked the friendliness of the people, nearly all of whom were eager to be helpful; and they liked the easy informality that characterized daily life. Accustomed to living in a genteel environment, they were pleased to discover that Clarksburg, despite its small size and relative youth, possessed culture and refinement. Richard Despard opened a store and for years was a successful merchant.

Among the children was a son named Burton, born in New York on January 28, 1816. In his new home he quickly made friends who introduced him to the wonders of the town and he surrounding countryside. The West Fork River and Elk Creek could be swum, fished, and in winter, skated upon. The encircling hills could be climbed; and from their tops, one could look down on the town which appeared remote and Lilliputian. In the wooded areas a boy could hunt with great success, for they abounded with small game. The court house, located near his father's store, dominated the town and was often visited by boys who liked watching people come and go as they transacted business. Some people, though, came just to visit with friends, tell exaggerated stories to anyone who would listen, o to trade such items as knives, watches, and horses. Young Despard, however, had chores assigned to him by his parents; and as he grew older, these increased so that he had little time to spend as he wished.

The Despards were Episcopalians and did much to promote their faith in their new home. From 1834 to 1837 the Rev. William Norvel Ward ministered to the town's small Episcopalian community and stayed part of that time with the Despards. Richard Despard did not live to see an Episcopal Church built in Clarksburg, but shortly after his death one was built on Main Street on land deeded by his son Burton. Designed to resemble the church the Despards had attended in Ireland, it is still standing and is today one of Clarksburg's most significant landmarks.

In his old age Richard Despard lived with his son-in-law and daughter Josiah and Mary Wilson; in their home this venerable son of Erin died on St. Patrick's Day, 1853, at the age of eighty-four. He was survived by his two sons, Richard, Jr., and Burton; his daughter, Mrs. Wilson; and several grandchildren. He was predeceased by his wife, by his daughter Charlotte, who had married Granville Davisson, and by other children.

84

Burton Despard had already become a leading citizen in the town by the time of his father's death. He had received his advanced education at Kenyon College in Ohio and in 1852 qualified before the Harrison County Bar. Around 1857 he associated himself with Edwin Maxwell in the practice of law. By then Clarksburg had long been noted for its capable lawyers whose services were sought by people from a wide area. Despard and his partner were popular and enjoyed a profitable practice that made them well-known far beyond the confines of the town.

Despard did not limit his activities to the legal profession, though, for young in life he had become involved in business as he helped his father operate the store and mange the family's investments. Realizing his son's capabilities, Richard Despard had gradually let him assume much of the responsibility for the family fortune, particularly after advancing years caused a decline in health. Despard also concerned himself with the acquisition of real estate and astutely acquired numerous choice parcels that brought him increasing wealth as time passed.

He married twice. His first wife was Emily Smith, daughter of Abraham Smith, a prosperous Pruntytown merchant. She was a young lady of exceptional qualities and descended from a prominent New Jersey Quaker family. Her death occurred in 1857. A few years later he married his second wife, Gertrude Lee, daughter of Judge George Hay Lee.

Unlike some of his friends, Despard did not involve himself to any great extent in civic affairs that carried with them time-consuming obligation. However, he did serve a term as the town's clerk and in 1853 was chosen one of the several commissioners to build a new court house, the county's third. When completed, this court house was an attractive two story structure crowned by a cupola and boasting a wrought iron balcony over its main entrance.

In 1860 Despard was among those who were responsible for the establishment of the town's second bank and for years took an active role in directing its policies. Originally a branch of a Wheeling bank, it in 1865 became an independent banking institution and assumed the name of Merchants National Bank. For a time it was the town's only bank and was of major importance to both Clarksburg and Harrison County. Its success was largely due to the guidance it received from such men as Despard.

During the Civil War, Despard, a slaveholder, was accused by some of being a Southern Sympathizer and was closely watched. This accusation, however was untrue, for he was among the town's leading men who in January 1861, declared themselves loyal to the federal government. The war brought many changes to the town, not a few of which were annoying to the inhabitants. It surely must have been very annoying to Despard to have Union soldiers build stables and a corral for horses and braying mules across the road from the mansion he had built in the 1850's. (this mansion , located on East Main Street, is one of Clarksburg's finest ante-bellum houses. It passed from the Despard family long-ago and for years has been a funeral home.)

Annoying too, must have been the crude behavior demonstrated by many soldiers, who all too often were loud and uncouth on the streets, and the attitude assumed by some of the officers who had only disparaging remarks to make about the town and its people. Finally, the war was over; and there was a quick return to normalcy. Despard and a host of other Clarkburgers must have sighed with relief.

Much of his land was underlaid with coal, and he became one of the area's pioneer coal developers. Throughout the 1850's and 1860's coal had steadily increased in importance, partly due to the fact that the railroad which reached the town a few years before the Civil War made possible large shipments t eastern markets. The Despard Mines, located near the town, attracted much attention and proved to be of considerable importance in the local economy. In 1866 Despard hired a young native of Philadelphia, Mordecai Lewis, as superintendent of his mines. He held the position for thirty-five years, married Luther Haymond's daughter, Myra, and in time became one of the town's best-known citizens.

The nineteenth century was a period of nearly unbelievable industrial development in the United States and witnessed a great number of innovations that made everyday living better. One such innovation was the use of manufactured gas for illumination. As far back as 1816 gas lights had been installed in a Philadelphia theater. Between then and 1870 there had been much improvement in gas burners, resulting in gas illumination becoming common in urban areas. In 1871 the Clarksburg Gas Company was organized with Despard as vice president. A plant was constructed on Monticello Avenue, and the first gas was produced from coal on January 19,1872. For a number of years the company supplied gas for the town's street lights and also the lamplighters who tended them.

In 1871 and 1872 Despard built a business block on property he owned at the corner of Main and South Third Streets. This was a costly project at a time when economic conditions were unsettled and was evidence of his faith in the town's future.

In January, 1874, he sold the Bridgeport Mill, which he had owned from 1854 to 1859 and from 1864 until the time he disposed of it. This important mill he had first acquired on January 23, 1854, from Joseph Johnson, then serving as governor of Virginia. According to one source, the mill dated to the 1780's and had been built by James Anderson, second sheriff of the county. In 1802 Ephraim Smith became its owner. Eventually, it passed into the possession of Smith's son-in-law, Joseph Johnson, who in 1849 rebuilt it.

The rebuilt mill was much larger and better than the old one and was not only equipped to saw wood and grind grist but also to card wool and spin yarn. Despard, of course, employed others to operate it during his ownership but no doubt assumed as active role in its management. It was for a long time one of Harrison County's outstanding mills.

In his last years Despard was plagued by failing health, a fact which brought frustration as he was forced to limit his activities and depend more and more upon others. On October 2, 1874, he died after having suffered a paralytic stroke.

Despard's widow later left Clarksburg and established her home in Philadelphia where she resided for years with her bachelor son, Duncan Lee Despard, a physician in that city. However, she maintained a close relationship with Clarksburg relatives and occasionally returned to visit them. A great niece has fond memories of her and her son and recalls with pleasure being a guest in their Philadelphia home. Although she outlived her husband for more than half a century, Mrs. Despard never remarried and, in the manner of a grand Victorian lady, dressed in the dark colors deemed proper for widowhood. She died in 1925.

Despard had several children by his two wives, one of whom was a daughter named Laura Ellen (1842-1918). In 1865 she married Nathan Goff Jr., who had served with distinction as a Union officer in the Civil War. He joined Despard's law firm and was of great assistance to him when his health began to fail. A truly outstanding son of Clarksburg, Goff rendered invaluable service to his state and nation in a career that included membership in both the House of Representatives and the United States senate.

Abstract of Memoranda

The following abstract was compiled by the editor. It attempts to identify which individuals Ms. Despard is referring to and what events they are party to. The page numbers are from the original manuscript, not the published text. The original text, some as scanned to OCR and some as transcribed, in blocks of original page numbers, can be obtained from the editor, Payton Despard Fireman. The abstract and addendum to the abstract, follows the Despard family tree, at least the American branch, through 2016 with at least basic information about the individual descendants.

Abstract of Jane Despard's Memoranda

Jane Despard's Memoranda was written by her in 1838 and addressed to her nephew Phillip Henry Despard (O'Brien) who is the son of Jane's brother William. Jane was residing at the time in Cheltenham, England.

First, the most frequently mentioned individuals that generate confusion in the text are:

Jane's Great Grandfather who is William Despard.

Jane's Grandfather, also William Despard (William of Donore).

Jane's Father, Philip Despard , who has the same name as her nephew.

Jane's nephew, Philip Henry Despard, to whom the memo is addressed.

Philip Henry's father William Despard, who is Jane's brother and father of her nephew, Philip Henry Despard.

I have done my best to insert the first names of these individuals where Jane has simply used the relationsip, father, grandfather, etc.

Ancient family history: One Phillip De Spar or Desparre, fled Charles IX as Protestant persecuted. St. Bartholomew Pogrom. He settled at Cranagh in Queens County, 1641.

Jane's Great Grandfather and His Brothers, Jane's Great-Great Uncles.

Jane's Great Grandfather William Despard Born, 1680 - Buried in Cloneagh churchyard. P.98 Unknown year on P.98 but earlier mentioned as Died In 1720 at Killaghy P. 10 Married in 1708 P. 7. To eldest co-heiress of Major Green, a Ms. Frances Green of Killaghy Castle. More P.8 He built Coleraine at an odd place because he had a better place called Middlemount nearby. Per Jane "Coleraine is not a pretty place." During last illness, told his wife to marry Councilor Hughes, one of the Guardians of his children. She did. P.10 but he died in a year. She then married a third time to Baron Keating P. 13, "having had two good husbands she wanted to try one of a different description" P.13-14.

Great Grandfather William's Brothers: Jane's Great Great Uncles.

1. Richard (of Cranagh) Guardian to Jane's Grandfather William P.10 Lived at Cranagh. P.98 Sent his nephew, Ward, William, to Eaton. Stole some of his money. P.10 P.13 P.98 Killed in a fall from a horse P. 100.

2. George, married Ms. Carden. Sixteen children, only eight survived. 40 year lawsuit P.104.

3. Also, Jane refers to older sister who marries Mr. Walsh. P. 10 Jane refers to two sisters, unnamed.

Jane's Grandfather & Great Uncles

1. William, Grandfather, Born 1711

2. Francis Great Uncle, Born 1712?

3. Rev. Richard P.97 Great Uncle Born 1714 –1720?

That is all for sons P.97,

Daughters

Mrs. Philips P. 82 P.97

Mrs. Metford (Mitford) P.82 P. 97

Mrs. Palmer P.82. P. 97

These women need to be born before 1720. Not likely from narrative. Six children in a twelve year marriage, is possible. Unless they are children of third husband Baron Keating

1. William Despard, Jane's Grandfather, Born 1711. Jane's grandfather married Ms. Walsh P.16, (her grandfather?) was from an ancient popish family in Howel Castle now Hoel or Hoyle, in County of Kilkenny, Part of this family supported Stuarts and sustained forfeitures. But Walsh's father worked for Cromwell P. 17 More Walshs P. 19

Had 9 children with Ms. Walsh 7 Boys 2 Girls P.23

Jane remembers being held by him as a child Jane Born 1790.

2. Francis of Killaghy, Owned and lived in Killaghy Castle, P. 69-70 Tipperary County P. 109 He is Great Grandfather to Kate of Killaghy P. 69. Money making man, Barrister but more intent on improving landed possessions than pleading at the bar. Died P.73 Married three times. P.70 Last one named Miss Cooke. Second Wife had son who died early. First wife who had two children that survived:

1. Unnamed Daughter P.70

2. Eldest son William P.71 Ran off to Scotland with older woman Ms. Clutterbuck @ 18 years old. P.71 Estranged from father till age 30. Associated with Clutterbucks, magistrate of county. A stern but negligent father. Died holding a volume of Shakespeare in his hand P. 72 & 75 Wife dies early P. 72. William remarries a widow, Ms. Sadleir (Stadler) P.73. 3rd time P. 75 To Ms. Short.

1. Francis, eldest son of William Studied for college. P.74 Like his father, he ran off with a woman to Dublin. P.74. Married her, Ms. Lecky. Francis inherited Killaghy Castle P.75

Francis had children. Foolishly Idolized children P. 78

1. Eldest Son unnamed, broke his hip in youth, died at 18. P.77

2. John, Very Handsome P.77 P.78 Dissipation

3. Thomas Intended for Doctor, died at 17 in an accident . P.77

4. Kate P. 77 Abducted and married P. 79 She did not go to India to marry. Married Mr. Wright, No child. Alive in 1838 P.82 P.83 Mr. Wright changed his name to Despard when he married Kate. P.83.

2. Thomas intended for attorney. P. 76 Hung out with Uncle Clutterbuck P. 76 Useless but respected P.76 Outlived his father William or else his uncles would not be Clutterbucks, No children Life estate to wife then to brother James with small legacy to his niece Kate.

3. James son P. 75. Father Rev. Francis prepared him for college. Became Pastor, became curate and earns 150 Pounds a year. Apparently alive in 1838

Jane's Great Uncle Rev. Richard, Third Son of William

3. Rev. Richard, P.83 Was a Clergyman. Lived at Mountrath. Married Ms. Burton of Burton Hall P.84. Died of Gout. P.84

Settled at Larch Hill near Coleraine. Left 5 boys 2 girls. Ms. Burton described again P. 92 had stroke but still awoke and read bible each day. He had 5 sons 2 daughters with Ms. Burton:

1. William, P. 85 Studied for Bar or medicine, Died in London

2. Francis See Below

3. Thomas Burton Despard P. 92 Present at capture of Jamaica, Year ?

4. Samuel P. 93 Married Ms. McMahon, Fled to America after shooting at creditors. Returned and died. Also P. 111-112. His widow, unnamed, P.94-95. 1838 Closing wretched life.

Jane's 2nd cousin Richard son of Jane's great uncle rev. Richard

5. Richard P. 96 Was in National Bank, Security for Samuel, Ruined. Fled to America, returned, paid debts and married Samuel's younger sister. P. 96. Her name was Diana McMahon. This is the Richard who emigrated to America and died in Harrison County in 1853 at 84 years old, born 1769. The only fly in the ointment is that Richard's father, by Jane's recollections died before 1760. The confirmation of his being Richard Despard is Jane's recollection of Richard returning to Ireland, paying debts and marrying the younger sister of his elder brother Samuel, who married a McMahon. Diana McMahon was the wife of the Richard Despard who lived in Clarksburg and he did return to Ireland to marry her, per Jack Sandy Anderson's Despard history. This corroboration is well nigh conclusive that this individual is our ancestor.

6. Eldest Daughter unnamed, married ploughman from the house. P. 85

7. 2nd daughter described P.93 but not named. Took care of Mom, Ms. Burton.

2nd Son Rev. Francis Despard, P.85 Pastor of church at Annatrim. Is Jane's Uncle. Married, "neither advantageously nor happily" Ms. Humphries, granddaughter of coachman at Coleraine. Their son, Unnamed, a gentleman attorney, He ran away with daughter of Captain John Despard of Cardtown. P.85, Rev. Francis beautified Larch Hill. Rev. Francis remarried Jane Despard AKA Mrs. Parson Despard P. 86. She had five Sons, at the birth of the last, she did not survive.

1. Richard, 23rd dragoons P. 87. Marries Ms. Olphits P. 88 Militia Paymaster, Ruins family P.90 This is 3-4 years before his father's death in 1819 P.90 American ancestor Richard is one generation prior. And his son, Richard, is not our Richard P.91 who got house.

2. Unnamed 2nd son died a midshipman in Royal Navy P.90

3. William, in iron business, declined and died P.90

4. Unnamed 4th son went to America to join uncle in business P.90

5. Frank, " wild man of the woods" Revenue agent, alive when Jane writes her memo in 1838

Rev. Francis married, 3rd wife P.88 She gave Rev. Francis an expensive funeral P.89. He died in 1819 P. 89 His grave is at Mountrath. His widow got a life estate in Larch Hill and then it went to Rev. Francis Eldest Grandson who is also Richard Despard. P.91 Else Richard's creditors would have taken it. Now, 1838, Larch Hill, is neglected and leased to a farmer.

Francis's Eldest Son Richard: P. 87 Was put in 23rd Dragoons then Richard really messed up the family finances. As paymaster of Dublin Militia had deficient accounts. His father, Rev. Francis, was security. Richard went to debtors prison accompanied by his father. His father paid 3,000 pounds in debts and evidently got him out of gaol. He then went to military prison and then escaped to America. After that his dad, Rev. Francis, had a fit whenever a letter arrived. He died four years later, a broken man, in 1819 @ 63 years of age. Jane, the Author, was with him then helping him and living in the area.

Using poor judgement Cousin Frank wanted to go out to dinner the night Rev. Francis, died. Jane, Author, said no. She does not like Frank. P. 65. Frank, "organ of destructiveness" threw out letters from Lord Talbot on politics.

Jane's Grandfather: P. 23 "Grandfather Despard"

Eldest Son of Jane's Great Grandfather, William Despard, was again, William Despard, he was Jane's Grandfather Owned Cardtown P.86 Born 1711 was 9 years old in 1720 when his father William died. Sent to Eton P.13. His Uncle, Richard, (his father's brother, not his brother Rev. Richard) was Guardian to Jane's grandfather. P.98 Cheated Jane's grandfather P.6.

Jane's Father, Uncles and Aunts:

1. Catherine, Aunt Kitty P.50. Born 1740?

2. William Oldest Son Sent to School Early P.23-24. Referred to by Jane as Uncle Despard" had a great wit. P.66 P. 85. Married Miss Armstrong of Gillon. Seven children. Peter, Frank,(died 1836)

3. Philip, Jane's father, 2nd son, sent to school early 23. P.66-69.

4. Cartrite named for Dr. Cartrite died unmarried P.51

5. Green, died unmarried, P. 51 Captain in Navy friend of Lord Longford, had illegitimate son P.53 Uncle Green P. 67 Fond of Music, a true sailor, "a man of taste with all of a sailor's feelings" Rustic Song about him. "Despard the knave, That son of the Wave."

6. John, called General John P.53, died 1817 P. 55 Had illegitimate son now Col. Hassard of Royal Engineers. Married Harriet P.57 the eldest sister of Sir Thomas Hesketh, Bart., of Rufford (Rumford) Hall,

7. Jane P. 56 Died young at 20, beautiful and loved. Jane of Colerain P.71

8. Andrew, died a Colonel, P. 56 –58-59 unmarried, 2 illegitimate children. Now, 1838, living with niece Ms. Pim. considered the Eucharist a papist ceremony. P. 66

9. Edward Marcus, P. 59 Most Talented in family, mapped Jamaica, Had black mistress, P. 61 Fought Duel P. 64 Tangled with Pitt. P. 61 Died unmarried. Governor of Natal and Superintendent of the coast of Honduras

Jane's Father & Mother:

Jane's Father, Philip Despard P. 23, P.34-35 & P.98. P.66-69. Was a great favorite of Grandfather William. Philip refused to be named eldest son. Was a bachelor till 38 P.36 Was in the army P.72. Jane's father died in 1817 P. 55 or 1818. As an older man with grown children. Went to Spain with General Smith P. 118 Born 1740? Married @38 in 1778? Died P.29 before the General did. 1817 P.55. Went to Downe's school to fit him for the army P. 33-35. Army Career Served in Gibraltar P.68 Retired on ½ pay. Wife, Jane's mother, Letitia Croasdale, at 38 years old. Jane's mother married to Philip in her house on Great Britain Street, Dublin. P.39. She and Philip lived near Rynn near Mountmellick for Military company for Philip. P.42 Then moved to Rirr. Jane was 5 at this time. Then moved to cottage of Uncle Despard near Laurel Hill. Family Ruined P. 44. Back to Dublin to live with mother in law. Back out to Country, terrorized by Whitefeet or Blackfeet, house burned, Plate stolen. Moved then to Mountmellick for protection then to Mountrath, where Jane's mother Letitia Croasdale died. P. 46 Philip was granted the Barrack Mastership of Monaghan and Philip died there P. 45.

1. Eliza Born 1789

2. Jane, the Author Born 1790 She would be 48 in 1838 when memo penned.

3. William, Eldest Son, Married Eliza Deblois

4. Philip, Chose Bad Profession P. 47 Went to West Indies, cleared his accounts with Government, cleared his securities. His widow has a pension. P.48. Phillip married first time to unnamed wife.

Phillip married to second wife Eliza, had issue.

1. Anne, died unmarried

2. Henry Parnell Moore, no issue, 2 marriages 2nd wife Jessie McDonald

3. Philippa, unmarried

4. Louisa, Married Alfred Charlton – no issue

5. Harriet, married Augustus Grantoff. 11 children

Jane's Nieces and Nephews – Brother Henry's Children. Henry, himself was a Major General and C.B. in the Army Was in India P.55 Died 1860.

Some of the following information recited was obtained from other sources; such a deeds, wills and family letters. Some persons are not referred to in Jane's text since they lived after her memo was completed.

1. Jane' Brother Henry, Married Anne Rushworth, had issue. One child, Sophia, married Arbuthnot Dallas who died in 1848. They had one daughter Annie

2. Frederick William Married Rosina Meredith, she died in 1858

   1. Daughter Frederika Mary

Frederick William Married again to Harriet Ann Nixon daughter of Dr. Nixon Bishop of Tasmania, had issue. Daughter Rosina

Jane's Nieces and Nephews, her brother William's children. He married Eliza Deblois, had issue.

1. Harriet - Married Thomas Murray of New Brunswick, had issue

    1. Francis

    2. Ellen

    3. Florence

2. Philip Henry to whom Jane writes the memo. Married Frances Anne O'Brien. Philip Henry died June 22nd, 1870 Philip is told that he is 5th generation of Killaghy Castle Direct descendant. Philip was given a legacy by his father William to Philip's brother George Packenham in preference to son of his sister, Eliza.(?) P.33 & P. 47. It appears that Philip Henry took the matrimonial name of O'Brien when he married Francis.

Philip Henry's children:

    1. William Edward who married Ellen daughter of Capt. Robertson R.N. William Edward may have changed his name or perhaps the editor is just incorrect because his children bear different last names. Had issue.

        1. Ellen Anne Robertson

        2. Frances Ethel Mary Robertson

        3. Philip O'Brien Robertson

    2. Frances Mary O'Brien

    3. Elizabeth Harriet Mary O'Brien

    4 Philip Hare O'Brien

    5. Letitia Emily O'Brien

6 Jessie Susan Anne O'Brien

Jane's Nieces and Nephews

Her brother Philip's children: Philip married to second wife
Eliza, had issue.

1. Anne, died unmarried

2. Henry Parnell Moore, no issue, 2 marriages 2nd wife Jessie
McDonald

3. Philippa, unmarried

4. Louisa, Married Alfred Charlton – no issue

5. Harriet, married Augustus Grantoff. 11 children, Harriet
Christina, Augustus Henry, Eliza Aujelia, Phillippa Matilda
Wright, Theresa Jane, Philip George Ludwig, Maria
Wilhemina Despard, Louisa Sophia, Bernand William, Ada
Georgina, Parnell Despard

Jane's first cousins children of uncle, William of Donore "Uncle
Despard". Also referred to as Uncle Despard is Mr. Despard
Croasdale. P.49.

Children of William of Donore and Ms. Armstrong of Gillon
P.25. Oldest son, of Jane's grandfather. William Despard
(William of Donore) P.23 Dublin University. Married Ms.
Armstrong. Had 7 Children. P. 31 Lived to 78 years old. 1740?
To 1818 about same time as Jane's father died in 1817.

1. (Philip) Peter Armstrong. Was Lt. in 18th, Dragoons, died of
fever. P. 25 Very young, no issue.

2. Frank, "Cross Grained" P. 26 Died 1836 P.25 P.30 P. 32 P.
61. Organ of destructiveness. Married Ms. Head, Left no issue.
Frank

3. Eliza, Married George Despard, P.27

4. William into Army died early "idle dissipated life" P. 26-27.

5. Mary, Married a Mr. Price of Lacka

Jane's First Cousins, children of Uncle John who married Harriet daughter of Hesketh of Rufford Hall, Lancashire who had issue

1. Harriet Died unmarried

2. Emma, married Lord Augustus Loftus (This is a real individual with a Wikipedia article)

3. Sophia died unmarried

4. Jessie Married John Horsley Palmer of London

5. Henry Fulke Grenville, Captain R.A.

6. Kate

William Wellesley Despard only one living in 1838 in Queen's Co. Has six sons and Four Daughters. P. 109

Addendum to Abstract

Following is an Addendum to the Abstract added by the editor, Payton D. Fireman relating to Despard descendants he is aware of, mostly from the American branch of the family.

According to Jane, the American Branch of the Despard family are all from Larch Hill.

Richard's Grandfather is the William Despard who is Jane's Great Grandfather.

Richard's Father is also Richard Despard. The Rev. Richard Despard. Which is Jane's Great Uncle.

Richard, son of Rev. Richard emigrated to America. He died on St. Patrick's Day, 1853, at the age of eighty-four. Tying him to Jane's memo, he was both Banker and security for his brother who had indigo business and then bought flour mills. Fled when the business collapsed and he was ruined, Returned to Ireland

and paid some debts and also Married Diana McMahon younger sister to his brother Samuel's wife. Had issue

1. Richard, Jr. survived father.

2. Mary Despard Wilson, Married Josiah Wilson, both survived Burton

3. Burton Despard, Born January 28th, 1816 in New York. Became lawyer, Died in 1874 of stroke. Married Emily Smith who died in 1857. Had issue:

    1. Laura Ellen Despard 1842-1918,

Burton subsequently married Gertrude Lee, daughter of Judge Lee, had issue, she survived until 1925. Had issue: Duncan Despard, Physician, lived in Philadelphia. Shot and killed by irate patient seeking to kill another doctor in his practice.

Laura Ellen Despard Married Nathan Goff Jr. Nathan became a United States Senator and Secretary of the Navy as well as serving as Justice on Fourth Circuit Court of Appeals for many years. Had issue.

1. Guy Despard Goff. Guy marries Louise Van Nortwick of Batavia Illinois, had one child, Louise Despard Goff, born 1898. Louise Married Brazilla Carrol Reese, who became a U.S. Congressman from Tennessee. Had issue: Carrol B. Reese

2. Waldo Percy Goff , who marries Caroline Basel, they have one child: Nathan Goff, III, who marries Catherine Osborn, has issue.

    1. Diana Goff, who marries Harold (H.) Dotson Cather, has issue.

        1. William Goff Cather Marries Cindy Hott, has issue:

            1. Lindsay Cather

2. Alexander Cather, deceased at 19 years old, 2014.

2. Laura Lyn Cather Pears, marries Daniel Pears, live in Texas, no issue.

3. Caroline Despard Cather Aras, marries John Aras, of Alexandria, Va., has issue:

1. Emily Aras

2. Evan Aras

2. The second child of Nathan Goff, III is Ms. Laura Ellen Goff. She marries Dr. Alfred Edmund Fireman, has issue: Payton Despard Fireman, Esq.

Laura Ellen, remarries to Shelly George Davis Phd, has one child.

1. Dr. Mary Diana Davis. Dr. Davis has two children.

1. Sophia Linn Luster, born 2008.

2. Lotus Ava Luster, born, 2010.

List of Notables

In addition to the comings and goings of the Despard family, Jane mentions interactions, relations to, and vignettes regarding a large number of individuals and families. Few are very dramatic, but all have the ring of truth and show the character of the persons involved in Janes's own particular idiom. Persons familiar with the historical period surveyed by Ms. Despard's memo may recognize several of the prominent people mentioned in her work. This list may serve as a shorthand way of placing the work in context to potential researchers looking for information about a particular time or subject matter.

Edward Marcus Despard
Lord Bantry
Lord Ross
Lord Longford
Lord Allen
Lord Townsend
Lord Cornwallis
Lord Hertford
Lord Belvidere
Lord Talbot
Lord Castlemaine
Lord Clancarty
Lord Hill
Lord Melbourne
Lord Maryborough
Lord Cavan
Lord Normanby
Lord Allen
Lord Rancliffe
Lord Gage
Lord Landaff
Lord Portarlington

Lord Mulgrave
Lord Norbury
Lord Gage
Lord Robert Bertie
Lady Longueville
Lady Clanbrassil
Lady Clarinda Trench
Lady Erne
Lady Levinge
Dowager Lady Southwell
Sir Thomas Hesketh
Sir Francis Burdett
Sir John Meridith
Sir Charles Coote
Sir John Carden
Sir George Pigott
Sir Richard Levinge
Sir John Kinasten
Sir Wm Pelly, ancestor to
the Marquis of Lansdown
Sir Thomas Burke
Baron Keating
General Crawford

General Slusser
General Marcus Smith
General Dunne
Baron Keating
The Nunn Family
Archbishop Boyle

Dowager Lady Southwell
Dean Swift
Walsh Family
Crossdale Family
O'Dowdal Family
Pim Family
Catherine Ryves
Rector of Blessington
Charles Fox's father
Colonel Guyllum
Colonel Prescott
William Pitt
Despard Croasdaile

Significant Places

Following is a list of place names, homes and other landmarks that are mentioned in the text.

Donore
Clonmel
Lismore in Queen's Co.
Larch Hill
Armagh
Killaghy Castle
Hill Castle, Wexford Co.
Cloneagh
Mountrath on road to Limerick
Castletown
Coleraine
Shanderry,
Rufford Hall, Lancashire
Laurel Hill, Built by Captain Green
Alta villa, Marquis of Lansdown.
Middlemount
Howel Castle "Now Hoel or Hoyle"
Rynn near Mountmellick
Gillon
Middlemount

Woodfert Iron Works
Bantry Estate
Mount Heaton near Roscrea
Shanderry
House at Rynn
Mountainstown in the County of Meath
Portarlington church
Brittas, not far from Rynn
Barraok Mastership of Monaghan
Church of Annatrim
Cardtown
Sir Charles Coote's Church
County Galway
County Armagh
County Tipperary
County Kilkenny
Queens County
County of Wicklow
County Meath
County of Kilkenny
County Galway

The following two descriptions of a place and person are included in their entirety and give a sense of Jane's narrative style:

Of the Welsh Hills Jane recites: Where "Castle Howel stands are called the Welsh hills to this day, they run along the river Barrow and into the Co. Waterford, on the borders of which river and on the edge of the two counties stand the beautiful ruins of the Abbey or Monastery of Rosbercon, erected early in the 14th century by Oliver Grace and Ursula Walsh."

Also; a Mr. Shekleton is described: He kept a "famous school of Ballitore, kept by a Quaker named Shekleton, who educated many famous men of that day, and among the rest the famous Edmund Burke, between whom and the son of Shekleton there commenced in boyhood a lasting friendship, and I have heard that his friend, Bradbourne, often appeared at the great dinners of Burke in London where he became a great man, and sometimes was accompanied by another Quaker of the name of Neal, also an old school-fellow."

Bibliography

https://en.wikipedia.org/wiki/Edward_Despard

https://en.wikipedia.org/wiki/Despard_Plot

Donore House, home to the Nugent family, was the largest estate in the area. It was sold to the Land Commission and the main house was demolished in the 1970s.

Jay, Mike, *The Unfortunate Colonel Despard* (Bantam Press 2004).

Oman, Charles William Chadwick. *Unfortunate Colonel Despard and Other Studies*. Burt Franklin, 1922.

Conner, Clifford D., *Colonel Despard: The Life and Times of an Anglo-Irish Rebel* Combined Publishing 2000.

Elliott, M., (1977). *The "Despard Conspiracy" Reconsidered. Past & Present,* (75), 46–61. Retrieved from JSTOR.

Jay, Mike. *The Unfortunate Colonel Despard*. Bantam Press, 2005.

Linebaugh, Peter, and Marcus Rediker, *The Many-Headed Hydra: Sailors, Slaves, Commoners, and the Hidden History of the Revolutionary Atlantica*, Beacon Press, 2013.

Porter, B. (1989). *Plots and paranoia: A history of political espionage in Britain, 1790–1988*. London ; Boston: Unwin Hyman.

Poole, S. (2000). *The politics of regicide in England, 1760–1850: Troublesome subjects*. Manchester : New York: Manchester University Press.

Smith, A. W. (1955). Irish Rebels and English Radicals 1798–1820. Past & Present, (7), 78–85. Retrieved from JSTOR.

Walsh, P. V. (2000). "Review of *Colonel Despard: The Life and Times of an Anglo-Irish Rebel*". The Journal of Military History, 64(4), 1153–1154.

Portrait of *Colonel Despard* published by Tegg & Co February 14th 1803. Author: Etching by Barlow (from sketch done at his trial) Source: https://pbs.twimg.com/media/CSy2tLmWIAAqEzE .jpg

References to Places and Homes

https://en.wikipedia.org/wiki/Donore,_County_Meath

https://en.wikipedia.org/wiki/Killagh_(civil_parish)

https://en.wikipedia.org/wiki/Nugent_baronets

https://en.wikipedia.org/wiki/Donore,_County_Westmeath

https://en.wikipedia.org/wiki/Despard,_West_Virginia

About the Editor

Payton D. Fireman is an attorney by trade and as of 2016 has practiced law in West Virginia for over thirty years.

In 1998 he founded The West Virginia Distilling Company, LLC, which is West Virginia's first legal distillery licensed since Prohibition. Payton was born in Boston in 1958 and raised in New York City as well as Lake Placid, New York. He attended high school in Clearwater, Florida. Moving to West Virginia in 1976 he completed his undergraduate and graduate studies at West Virginia University in 1983. Payton is a member of both the West Virginia and Florida Bar Associations. He was director of the Criminal Justice Program at Salem College from 1985 until 1989 and then served as a Trust Officer for Huntington Bank for ten years until establishing his private practice in 1997. In 1998 he began building his distillery.

His company websites are www.mountainmoonshine.com and www.alcoholblending.com.

Payton recently published a book on how to operate a small distillery under the title of *Distillery Operations*, ISBN: 978-0-9833376-4-5. The book's focus is on the actual mechanical, biological and chemical aspects of operating a distillery and outlines the procedures and processes necessary to produce quality beverage grade alcohol on a commercial but still artisanal scale. The later parts of the work are devoted to the author's experiences and conclusions about the distilling business.

https://www.amazon.com/Distillery-Operations-How-Run -Small/dp/0983337640/ref=sr_1_2?s=books&ie=UTF8 &qid=1466436047&sr=1-2&keywords=Distillery+Operations

In conjunction with the distillery operations book, Payton recently uploaded to his YouTube channel, MoonshineDistilling, a two hour video chronicling an entire year's production cycle at his distillery. This video complements the operations book by demonstrating the processes and procedures discussed in the book.

Distillery Operations Complete Video: https://youtu.be /4qAgrDDVHfo

Payton has also written, published and maintained two alcohol industry related computer programs.

1. Alcohol Blending Software: To improve upon the government regimen for alcohol blending and accounting, Alcohol Blending Software (ABS), is a program which can be used to manage virtually every part of a distiller's business.

http://mountainmoonshine.com/alcoholblendingsoftware /orderinginformation.html

2. Distillery Operations Workbook 1.0: This workbook contains all of the spreadsheets which were created in order to write the Distilling Operations textbook. The software is fully functional and users can modify the input values for each worksheet to meet their own particular needs.

http://mountainmoonshine.com/distilloperationsbook.html

Payton serves as the Trustee of the Melba Zinn Trust and in that capacity published a Kindle edition of Ms. Zinn's 12-volume work abstracting the county court records of Monongalia County from 1796 through 1824. Originally published as paperback books by Heritage Books the Kindle edition combines all twelve volumes into one searchable electronic edition.

https://www.amazon.com/Monongalia-Virginia-Records-District -Superior-ebook/dp/B01AY971CQ/ref=sr_1_1?s=books&ie =UTF8&qid=1466449856&sr=1-1&keywords=melba+zinn

Subjects include indictments, prosecutions, and verdicts; miscellaneous tax returns and ledgers; probate records, inventories; petitions to the courts; and many other civil and criminal matters.

Payton also recently edited and posthumously published his father's two books on psychotherapy.

1. *Unhitching from Bitching*: Dr. Alfred Fireman explains his views on the dynamics of interpersonal relationships in light of his experience in practicing psychiatry with particular attention to relationships with spouses, lovers, friends, grown children and parents. The work allows the reader to identify and inventory the behavioral mechanisms that create either loving or damaging relationships and, when necessary, to unhitch from relationships that are objectively not worth pursuing.

https://www.amazon.com/Unhitching-Bitching-Love-Lessons
-Psychotherapists/dp/0983337632/ref=sr_1_2?s=books&ie
=UTF8&qid=1466446629&sr=1-2&keywords=Alfred+Fireman

2. *Understanding Someone Else for a Change*: This work is a summary of many of the ways that people relate to one another and serves as a tool to learn how to identify why people behave in particular ways. While broadly speaking it is a self help book, it is more akin to reading a summary of the wisdom gained by years of practicing psychiatry with respect to what motivates people to certain behaviors.

https://www.amazon.com/Understanding-Someone-Else-Change
-Outsight/dp/0983337624/ref=sr_1_1?s=books&ie=UTF8&qid
=1466446629&sr=1-1&keywords=Alfred+Fireman

Payton Despard Fireman
Outside Warhol Museum, Pittsburgh, PA, 2010

www.ingramcontent.com/pod-product-compliance
Lightning Source LLC
Chambersburg PA
CBHW061748020426
42331CB00006B/1393